Reproducible Maps, Charts Time Lines & Illustrations

Regal

A Division of Gospel Light
Ventura, California, U.S.A.

ISBN 0-8307-1938-5
© 1989 by Gospel Light
All rights reserved.
Printed in U.S.A.

HOW TO MAKE CLEAN COPIES FROM THIS BOOK

Table of Contents

Introduction

When we find ourselves in unfamiliar surroundings we realize the need to become "oriented"—literally, to "face the east"—or find a fixed point in order to get our bearings. Especially when we are lost, correct orientation can be the first step toward finding our way home.

Christians honor the Bible as the book that shows a lost world the way home to God, yet this book is actually a whole library—a collection of 66 books, written over a period of 1,600 years. With such a broad landscape, it is possible to become disoriented in the Bible itself.

This resource is a Bible-orientation course. It enables you to face the east—this time the Middle East—in order to give a frame of reference to your Bible study. It helps you visualize the settings of Scripture with maps and charts, purpose/theme statements, main characters, outlines, time lines, illustrations and key verses—all to help you find your bearings in the vast expanse of God's Word.

Reproducible Maps, Charts, Time Lines and Illustrations draws together in a single resource the work of expert biblical graphics artist Hugh Claycombe and nutshell overviews of both the broad divisions and particular books of the Bible. This blend of exacting detail, simplified summaries and even historical cartoons make the guide adaptable to a wide range of age groups and levels of Bible knowledge. Claycombe's work is drawn from *The NIV Study Bible*—the version recommended for use with this resource.

Much of the information about the setting and purpose of the books of the Bible can be committed to memory, since it is presented in such a concise form. The simplified time lines are especially useful in helping the student recall how biblical people and their writings relate to other events around them. Since establishing the precise date of many books is difficult, the time lines focus more on the approximate dates of events, rather than the time of the writing of the book.

We pray that this Bible study resource book will serve as a helpful guide on your pilgrimage through God's Word, and on your way Home.

—The editors

How to Use This Book

Many people find it hard to concentrate on talks and texts about the Bible. *Reproducible Maps, Charts, Time Lines and Illustrations* captures and holds our attention with visual aids. It is especially valuable for group studies of the Bible. The pages are perforated to aid you in making quality photocopies of the material to be distributed to group members. We ask that you follow the "How to Make Clean Copies from This Book" guidelines found on the copyright page. The pages may also be used with an opaque projector or to make transparencies for use with an overhead projector.

If you are using a projector, don't forget the technique of covering part of a page with a blank sheet of paper to enable the group to focus on a particular section. For example, you may want to review a lesson on a particular book by covering the Purpose/Theme section and asking the group to recall the purpose or theme.

Reproducible Maps, Charts, Time Lines and Illustrations is also valuable for personal study. Some people are incurable reference book readers. They can't look up the spelling of one word without being drawn to a dozen others on the way. They can cozy up to an encyclopedia like others sit down with a novel. If this describes you, just enjoy *Reproducible Maps, Charts, Time Lines and Illustrations* as you would any other book with such a wealth of fascinating references.

A daily Bible reading plan would also be enhanced with this book. Its maps and time lines can help you keep in mind the historical setting of the text. The summaries and key verses can remind you of the main thrust of each book and keep you from missing the forest for the trees. You can refer to lists such as "Major Archeological Finds Relating to the New Testament" to see the progress researchers have made in discovering the setting of Scripture. The Purpose/Theme statements and the key verses provide useful supplements to the habit of memorizing favorite passages of Scripture.

In whatever setting you use this resource, take advantage of the *visual* impact of this material, allowing it to lend to Bible study something of the concrete reality in which Scripture originally appeared.

The Old Testament Bookshelf

The word "testament" means "will" or "covenant." The term "Old Testament," therefore, refers first to God's covenant or promise-law to bless mankind through the Jewish nation. It has also come to refer to the *writings about* the Old Covenant, although, strictly speaking, these ancient books are the Old Covenant *Scriptures.*

Purpose/Theme:

The Scriptures of the Old Testament record the story of God's chosen people, Israel, and their relationship to His covenant to bless all nations through them.

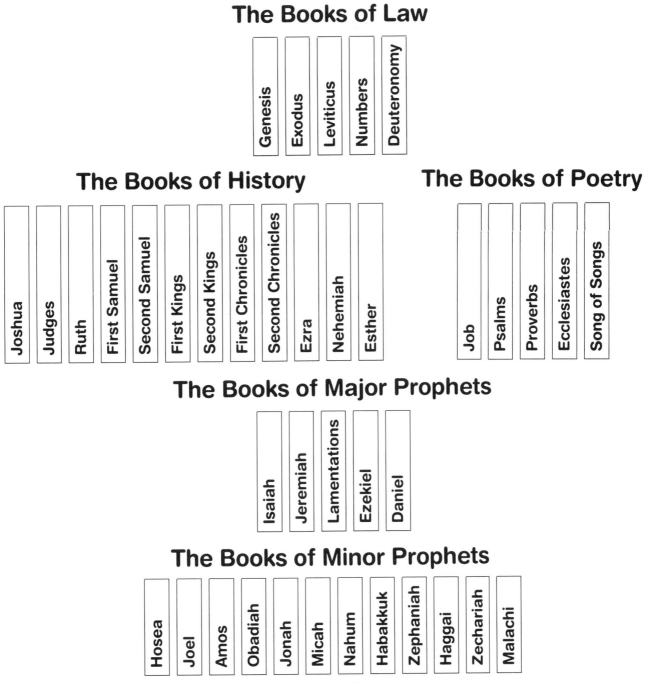

The Books of Law

Genesis, Exodus, Leviticus, Numbers, Deuteronomy

The Books of History

Joshua, Judges, Ruth, First Samuel, Second Samuel, First Kings, Second Kings, First Chronicles, Second Chronicles, Ezra, Nehemiah, Esther

The Books of Poetry

Job, Psalms, Proverbs, Ecclesiastes, Song of Songs

The Books of Major Prophets

Isaiah, Jeremiah, Lamentations, Ezekiel, Daniel

The Books of Minor Prophets

Hosea, Joel, Amos, Obadiah, Jonah, Micah, Nahum, Habakkuk, Zephaniah, Haggai, Zechariah, Malachi

When Old Testament Events Happened

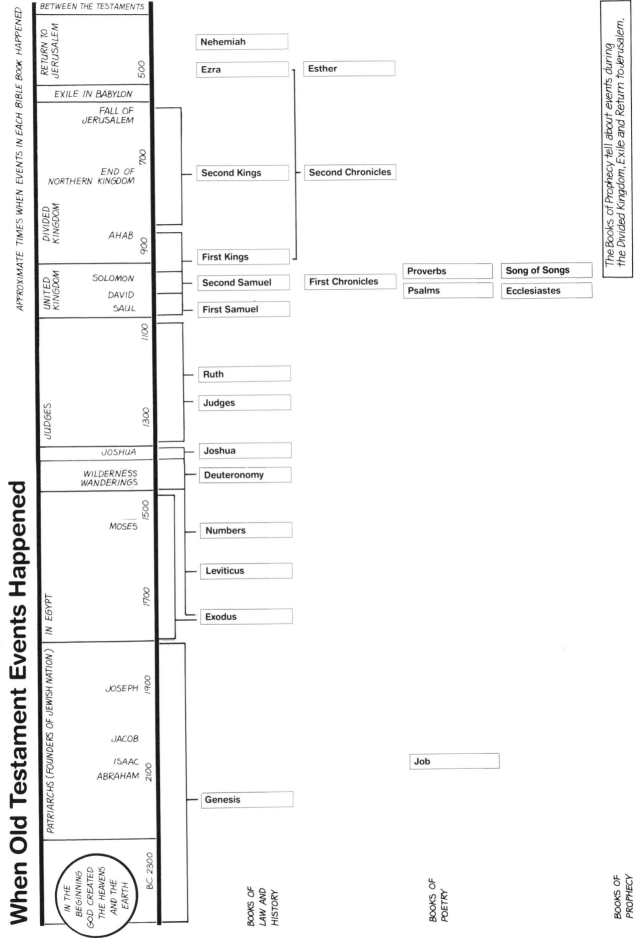

APPROXIMATE TIMES WHEN EVENTS IN EACH BIBLE BOOK HAPPENED

BETWEEN THE TESTAMENTS

RETURN TO JERUSALEM

500

EXILE IN BABYLON

FALL OF JERUSALEM

700

END OF NORTHERN KINGDOM

DIVIDED KINGDOM

AHAB

900

UNITED KINGDOM

SOLOMON

DAVID

SAUL

1100

JUDGES

1300

JOSHUA

WILDERNESS WANDERINGS

1500

MOSES

1700

IN EGYPT

JOSEPH

1900

JACOB

ISAAC

ABRAHAM

2100

PATRIARCHS (FOUNDERS OF JEWISH NATION)

BC 2300

IN THE BEGINNING GOD CREATED THE HEAVENS AND THE EARTH

Nehemiah

Ezra

Esther

Second Kings

Second Chronicles

First Kings

Second Samuel

First Chronicles

Proverbs

Song of Songs

Psalms

Ecclesiastes

First Samuel

Ruth

Judges

Joshua

Deuteronomy

Numbers

Leviticus

Exodus

Job

Genesis

BOOKS OF LAW AND HISTORY

BOOKS OF POETRY

BOOKS OF PROPHECY

The Books of Prophecy tell about events during the Divided Kingdom, Exile and Return to Jerusalem.

Books of Law

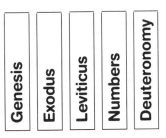

The five books of the Law are also called "the Pentateuch," which means "five scrolls." At least some of this ancient literature was written by Moses (Luke 24:27, John 5:46). These books describe the creation of the world, God's call to the Hebrews to be His special people, their captivity and release from Egypt, the laws which guided them on their way to the Promised Land and how God blessed the people when they obeyed and disciplined them when they disobeyed.

When Events Happened

Genesis

Books of the Law

Genesis | Exodus | Leviticus | Numbers | Deuteronomy

Purpose/Theme:

Genesis (which means "the beginning") records the creation of the world and of the Jewish nation.

Key Verses:

"God saw all that he had made, and it was very good" (1:31).

"The Lord had said to Abram, 'Leave your country, your people and your father's household and go to the land I will show you. I will make you into a great nation and I will bless you . . . and all peoples on earth will be blessed through you" (12:1,2,3).

Main People:

Adam and Eve; Noah; Abraham, Isaac and Jacob; Joseph.

Outline:

☐ The creation of the world (Genesis 1,20)
☐ Sin in the world (Genesis 3,4)
☐ Noah and the flood (Genesis 5—9)
☐ The beginning of nations and languages (Genesis 10,11)
☐ Abraham's family: God's people in the land God gave them (Genesis 12—38)
☐ Joseph: God's people going to Egypt (Genesis 39—50)

When Events Happened

FLOOD   BABEL   ABRAHAM   ISAAC

JACOB   JOSEPH

Table of Nations

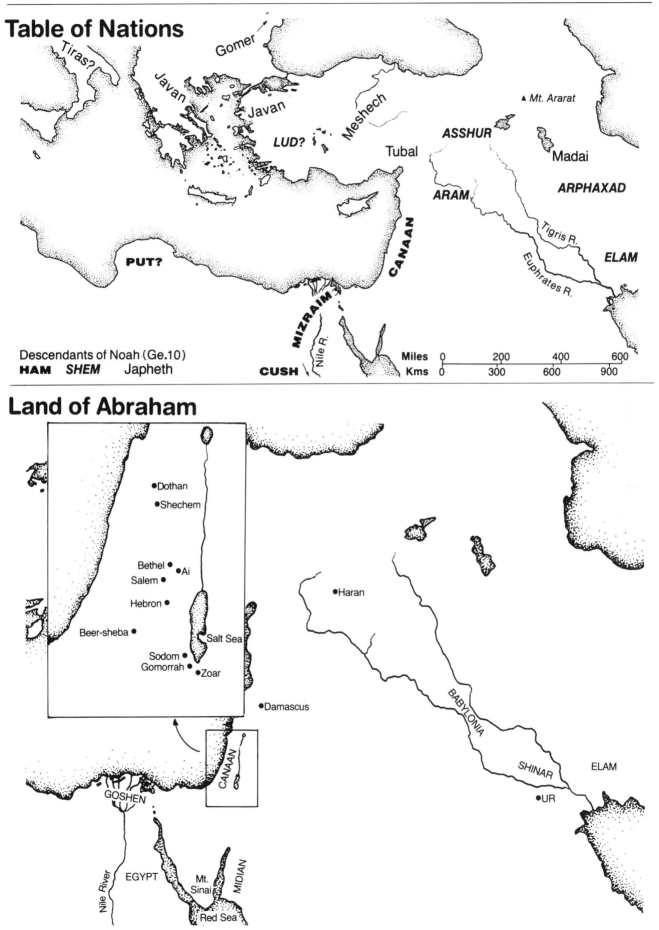

Tiras?
Gomer
Javan
Javan
Meshech
LUD?
Tubal
▲ Mt. Ararat
ASSHUR
Madai
ARAM
ARPHAXAD
Tigris R.
Euphrates R.
ELAM
PUT?
CANAAN
MIZRAIM
CUSH
Nile R.

Descendants of Noah (Ge.10)
HAM *SHEM* Japheth

Miles	0	200	400	600
Kms	0	300	600	900

Land of Abraham

●Dothan
●Shechem
Bethel ● ●Ai
Salem ●
Hebron ●
Beer-sheba ●
Salt Sea
Sodom ●
Gomorrah ● ●Zoar
●Damascus
●Haran
BABYLONIA
SHINAR
ELAM
●UR
CANAAN
GOSHEN
Nile River
EGYPT
Mt. Sinai
MIDIAN
Red Sea

Jacob's Journey

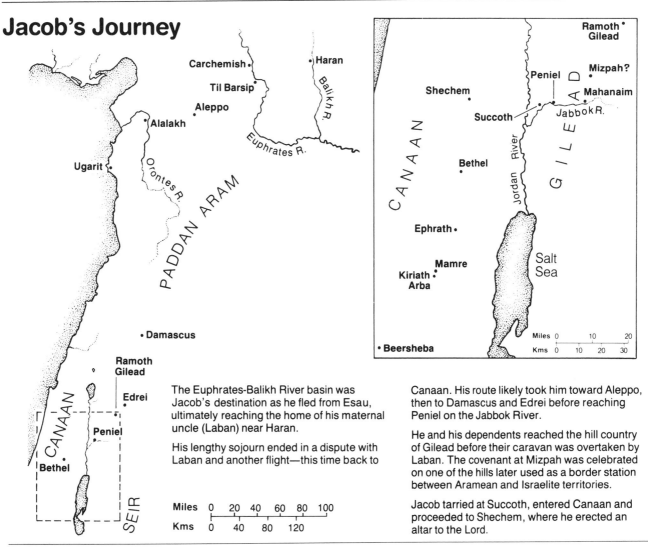

The Euphrates-Balikh River basin was Jacob's destination as he fled from Esau, ultimately reaching the home of his maternal uncle (Laban) near Haran.

His lengthy sojourn ended in a dispute with Laban and another flight—this time back to Canaan. His route likely took him toward Aleppo, then to Damascus and Edrei before reaching Peniel on the Jabbok River.

He and his dependents reached the hill country of Gilead before their caravan was overtaken by Laban. The covenant at Mizpah was celebrated on one of the hills later used as a border station between Aramean and Israelite territories.

Jacob tarried at Succoth, entered Canaan and proceeded to Shechem, where he erected an altar to the Lord.

The Tribes of Israel

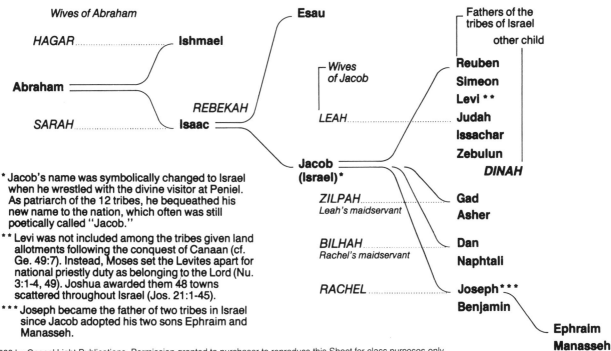

* Jacob's name was symbolically changed to Israel when he wrestled with the divine visitor at Peniel. As patriarch of the 12 tribes, he bequeathed his new name to the nation, which often was still poetically called "Jacob."

** Levi was not included among the tribes given land allotments following the conquest of Canaan (cf. Ge. 49:7). Instead, Moses set the Levites apart for national priestly duty as belonging to the Lord (Nu. 3:1-4, 49). Joshua awarded them 48 towns scattered throughout Israel (Jos. 21:1-45).

*** Joseph became the father of two tribes in Israel since Jacob adopted his two sons Ephraim and Manasseh.

Exodus

Books of the Law

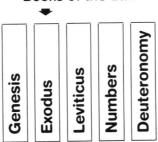

| Genesis | Exodus | Leviticus | Numbers | Deuteronomy |

Purpose/Theme:

To record the Exodus (or "departure") of the Jews from Egyptian bondage.

Key Verse:

"I have come down to rescue them from the hand of the Egyptians and to bring them up out of that land into a good and spacious land, a land flowing with milk and honey" (3:8).

Main People:

Pharaoh; Moses and his brother, Aaron.

Outline:

☐ The slavery of God's people (Exodus 1)
☐ The call of Moses to be the leader of God's people (Exodus 2—4)
☐ The challenge for Pharaoh to release God's people (Exodus 5—11)
☐ The passover for God's people—a picture of Jesus as our Savior (Exodus 12,13)
☐ The exodus of God's people from Egypt (Exodus 14—19)
☐ The giving of the Law to God's people (Exodus 20—24)
☐ The building of the Tabernacle by God's people (Exodus 25—40)

When Events Happened

1600 BC   *1400 BC*

MOSES

Hebrew Calendar and Selected Events

NUMBER of MONTH		HEBREW NAME	MODERN EQUIVALENT	BIBLICAL REFERENCES	AGRICULTURE	FEASTS
1	Sacred sequence begins	Abib; Nisan	MARCH—APRIL	Ex 12:2; 13:4; 23:15; 34:18; Dt 16:1; Ne 2:1; Est 3:7	Spring (later) rains; barley and flax harvest begins	Passover; Unleavened Bread; Firstfruits
2		Ziv (Iyyar)*	APRIL—MAY	1 Ki 6:1, 37	Barley harvest; dry season begins	
3		Sivan	MAY—JUNE	Est 8:9	Wheat harvest	Pentecost (Weeks)
4		(Tammuz)*	JUNE—JULY		Tending vines	
5		(Ab)*	JULY—AUGUST		Ripening of grapes, figs and olives	
6		Elul	AUGUST—SEPTEMBER	Ne 6:15	Processing grapes, figs and olives	
7	1 Civil sequence	Ethanim (Tishri)*	SEPTEMBER—OCTOBER	1 Ki 8:2	Autumn (early) rains begin; plowing	Trumpets; Atonement; Tabernacles (Booths)
8	2	Bul (Marcheshvan)*	OCTOBER—NOVEMBER	1 Ki 6:38	Sowing of wheat and barley	
9	3	Kislev	NOVEMBER—DECEMBER	Ne 1:1; Zec 7:1	Winter rains begin (snow in some areas)	Hanukkah ("Dedication")
10	4	Tebeth	DECEMBER—JANUARY	Est 2:16		
11	5	Shebat	JANUARY—FEBRUARY	Zec 1:7		
12	6	Adar	FEBRUARY—MARCH	Ezr 6:15; Est 3:7,13; 8:12; 9:1,15,17,19,21	Almond trees bloom; citrus fruit harvest	Purim
		(Adar Sheni)* Second Adar				

This intercalary month was added about every three years so the lunar calendar would correspond to the solar year.

* Names in parentheses are not in the Bible

The Exodus

The exodus and conquest narratives form the classic historical and spiritual drama of OT times. Subsequent ages looked back to this period as one of obedient and victorious living under divine guidance. Close examination of the environment and circumstances also reveals the strenuous exertions, human sin and bloody conflicts of the era.

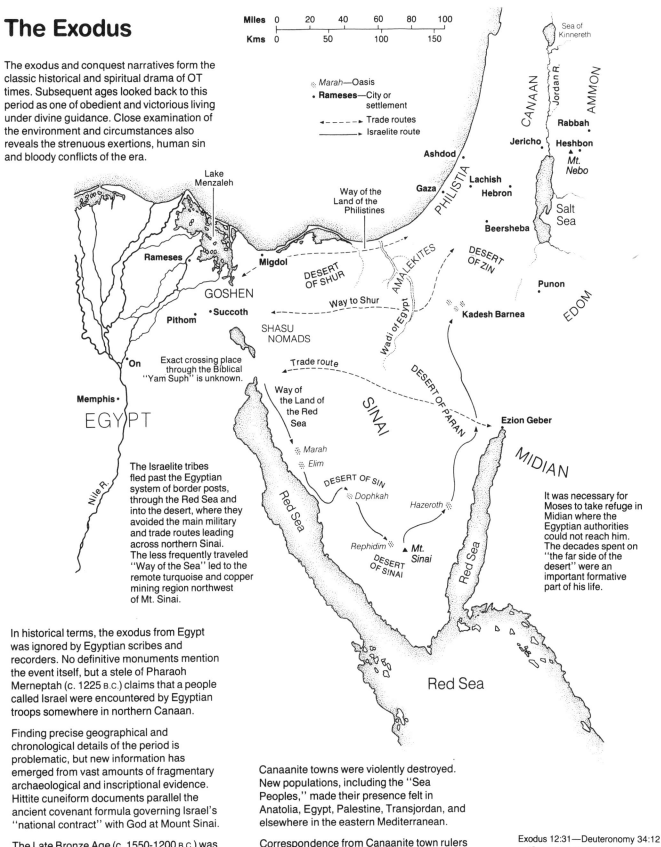

Miles 0   20   40   60   80   100

Kms 0   50   100   150

Marah—Oasis
Rameses—City or settlement
Trade routes
Israelite route

The Israelite tribes fled past the Egyptian system of border posts, through the Red Sea and into the desert, where they avoided the main military and trade routes leading across northern Sinai. The less frequently traveled "Way of the Sea" led to the remote turquoise and copper mining region northwest of Mt. Sinai.

It was necessary for Moses to take refuge in Midian where the Egyptian authorities could not reach him. The decades spent on "the far side of the desert" were an important formative part of his life.

In historical terms, the exodus from Egypt was ignored by Egyptian scribes and recorders. No definitive monuments mention the event itself, but a stele of Pharaoh Merneptah (c. 1225 B.C.) claims that a people called Israel were encountered by Egyptian troops somewhere in northern Canaan.

Finding precise geographical and chronological details of the period is problematic, but new information has emerged from vast amounts of fragmentary archaeological and inscriptional evidence. Hittite cuneiform documents parallel the ancient covenant formula governing Israel's "national contract" with God at Mount Sinai.

The Late Bronze Age (c. 1550-1200 B.C.) was a time of major social migrations. Egyptian control over the Semites in the eastern Nile delta was harsh, with a system of brickmaking quotas imposed on the labor force, often the landless, low-class "Apiru." Numerous

Canaanite towns were violently destroyed. New populations, including the "Sea Peoples," made their presence felt in Anatolia, Egypt, Palestine, Transjordan, and elsewhere in the eastern Mediterranean.

Correspondence from Canaanite town rulers to the Egyptian court in the time of Akhenaten (c. 1375 B.C.) reveals a weak structure of alliances, with an intermittent Egyptian military presence and an ominous fear of people called "Habiru" ("Apiru").

Exodus 12:31—Deuteronomy 34:12
(Summary: Numbers 33:1-48)

The Tabernacle

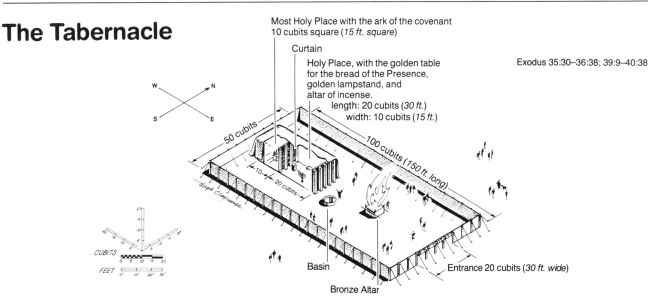

Most Holy Place with the ark of the covenant
10 cubits square (*15 ft. square*)

Curtain

Holy Place, with the golden table
for the bread of the Presence,
golden lampstand, and
altar of incense.
length: 20 cubits (*30 ft.*)
width: 10 cubits (*15 ft.*)

Exodus 35:30–36:38; 39:9–40:38

50 cubits

100 cubits (*150 ft. long*)

10 — 20 cubits

High Claycombe

CUBITS

FEET

Basin

Bronze Altar

Entrance 20 cubits (*30 ft. wide*)

The new religious observances taught by Moses in the desert centered on rituals connected with the tabernacle, and amplified Israel's sense of separateness, purity and oneness under the Lordship of Yahweh.

A few desert shrines have been found in Sinai, notably at Serabit el-Khadem and at Timnah in the Negev, and show marked Egyptian influence.

Specific cultural antecedents to portable shrines carried on poles and covered with thin sheets of gold can be found in

ancient Egypt as early as the Old Kingdom (2800-2250 B.C.), but were especially prominent in the 18th and 19th dynasties (1570-1180). The best examples come from the fabulous tomb of Tutankhamun, c. 1350.

Comparisons of construction details in the text of Ex 25-40 with the frames, shrines, poles, sheathing, draped fabric covers, gilt rosettes, and winged protective figures from the shrine of Tutankhamun are instructive. The period, the Late Bronze Age, is equivalent in all dating systems to the era of Moses and the exodus.   © Hugh Claycombe 1981

The Tabernacle Furnishings

Exodus 37–38:8

The symbolism of God's redemptive covenant was preserved in the tabernacle, making each element an object lesson for the worshiper. The Levitical priests, including some with Egyptian names and perhaps Egyptian training, gave meticulous attention to facts about the shrine. Reconstruction of the furnishings is possible because of extremely detailed descriptions and precise measurements recorded in Ex 25-40.

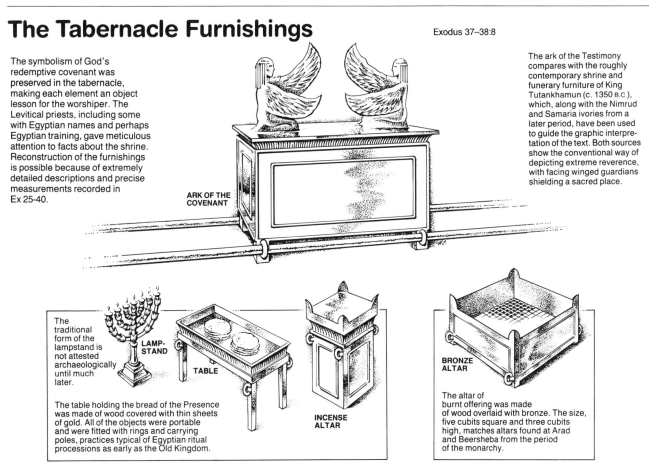

ARK OF THE
COVENANT

The ark of the Testimony compares with the roughly contemporary shrine and funerary furniture of King Tutankhamun (c. 1350 B.C.), which, along with the Nimrud and Samaria ivories from a later period, have been used to guide the graphic interpretation of the text. Both sources show the conventional way of depicting extreme reverence, with facing winged guardians shielding a sacred place.

The traditional form of the lampstand is not attested archaeologically until much later.

LAMP-STAND

TABLE

The table holding the bread of the Presence was made of wood covered with thin sheets of gold. All of the objects were portable and were fitted with rings and carrying poles, practices typical of Egyptian ritual processions as early as the Old Kingdom.

INCENSE
ALTAR

BRONZE
ALTAR

The altar of burnt offering was made of wood overlaid with bronze. The size, five cubits square and three cubits high, matches altars found at Arad and Beersheba from the period of the monarchy.

Leviticus

Books of the Law

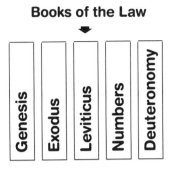

Purpose/Theme:
Named for Levi, head of the priestly tribe in Israel, this book records various laws and rituals, and the role of the priests, in the Jewish sacrificial system.

Key Verses:
"Consecrate yourselves and be holy, because I am the Lord your God. Keep my decrees and follow them. I am the Lord, who makes you holy" (20:7-8).

Main People:
The people who bring the offerings (people of God) and the people who sacrifice the offerings (priests).

Outline:
☐ **Sacrifice and Separation**—How can an unholy person come to a holy God? (Leviticus 1:1—6:7)
☐ **The Priest**—The priest went to God with the prayers and praises of the people. (Leviticus 8—10)
☐ **Rules About Daily Living** (Leviticus 11—22)
☐ **The Day of Atonement** (Leviticus 16)
☐ **The Feasts** (Leviticus 23—25)

When Events Happened

1600 BC   1400 BC

MOSES

Old Testament Sacrifices

NAME	OT REFERENCES	ELEMENTS	PURPOSE
BURNT OFFERING	Lev 1; 6:8-13; 8:18-21; 16:24	Bull, ram or male bird (dove or young pigeon for poor); wholly consumed; no defect	Voluntary act of worship; atonement for unintentional sin in general; expression of devotion, commitment and complete surrender to God
GRAIN OFFERING	Lev 2; 6:14-23	Grain, fine flour, olive oil, incense, baked bread (cakes or wafers), salt; no yeast or honey; accompanied burnt offering and fellowship offering (along with drink offering)	Voluntary act of worship; recognition of God's goodness and provisions; devotion to God
FELLOWSHIP OFFERING	Lev 3; 7:11-34	Any animal without defect from herd or flock; variety of breads	Voluntary act of worship; thanksgiving and fellowship (it included a communal meal)
SIN OFFERING	Lev 4:1-5:13; 6:24-30; 8:14-17; 16:3-22	1. Young bull: for high priest and congregation 2. Male goat: for leader 3. Female goat or lamb: for common person 4. Dove or pigeon: for the poor 5. Tenth of an ephah of fine flour: for the very poor	Mandatory atonement for specific unintentional sin; confession of sin; forgiveness of sin; cleansing from defilement
GUILT OFFERING	Lev 5:14-6:7; 7:1-6	Ram or lamb	Mandatory atonement for unintentional sin requiring restitution; cleansing from defilement; make restitution; pay 20% fine

When more than one kind of offering was presented (as in Nu 6:16, 17), the procedure was usually as follows: (1) sin offering or guilt offering, (2) burnt offering, (3) fellowship offering and grain offering (along with a drink offering). This sequence furnishes part of the spiritual significance of the sacrificial system. First, sin had to be dealt with (sin offering or guilt offering). Second, the worshiper committed himself completely to God (burnt offering and grain offering). Third, fellowship or communion between the Lord, the priest and the worshiper (fellowship offering) was established. To state it another way, there were sacrifices of expiation (sin offerings and guilt offerings), consecration (burnt offerings and grain offerings) and communion (fellowship offerings—these included vow offerings, thank offerings and freewill offerings).

Old Testament Feasts and Other Sacred Days

NAME	OT REFERENCES	OT TIME	MODERN EQUIVALENT	DESCRIPTION	PURPOSE	NT REFERENCES
Sabbath	Ex 20:8–11; 31:12–17; Lev 23:3; Dt 5:12–15	7th day	Same	Day of rest; no work	Rest for people and animals	Mt 12:1–14; 28:1; Lk 4:16; Jn 5:9; Ac 13:42; Col 2:16; Heb 4:1–11
Sabbath Year	Ex 23:10–11; Lev 25:1–7	7th year	Same	Year of rest; fallow fields	Rest for land	
Year of Jubilee	Lev 25:8–55; 27:17–24; Nu 36:4	50th year	Same	Canceled debts; liberation of slaves and indentured servants; land returned to original family owners	Help for poor; stabilize society	
Passover	Ex 12:1–14; Lev 23:5; Nu 9:1–14; 28:16; Dt 16:1–3a, 4b–7	1st month (Abib) 14	Mar.-Apr.	Slaying and eating a lamb, together with bitter herbs and bread made without yeast, in every household	Remember Israel's deliverance from Egypt	Mt 26:17; Mk 14:12–26; Jn 2:13; 11:55; 1Co 5:7; Heb 11:28
Unleavened Bread	Ex 12:15–20; 13:3–10; 23:15; 34:18; Lev 23:6–8; Nu 28:17–25; Dt 16:3b, 4a, 8	1st month (Abib) 15–21	Mar.-Apr.	Eating bread made without yeast; holding several assemblies; making designated offerings	Remember how the Lord brought the Israelites out of Egypt in haste	Mk 14:1,12; Ac 12:3; 1 Co 5:6–8
Firstfruits	Lev 23:9–14	1st month (Abib) 16	Mar.-Apr.	Presenting a sheaf of the first of the barley harvest as a wave offering; making a burnt offering and a grain offering	Recognize the Lord's bounty in the land	Ro 8:23; 1 Co 15:20–23
Weeks (Pentecost) (Harvest)	Ex 23:16a; 34:22a; Lev 23:15–21; Nu 28:26–31; Dt 16:9–12	3rd month (Sivan) 6	May-June	A festival of joy; mandatory and voluntary offerings, including the firstfruits of the wheat harvest	Show joy and thankfulness for the Lord's blessing of harvest	Ac 2:1–4; 20:16; 1Co 16:8
Trumpets (Later: Rosh Hashanah—New Year's Day)	Lev 23:23–25; Nu 29:1–6	7th month (Tishri) 1	Sept.-Oct.	An assembly on a day of rest commemorated with trumpet blasts and sacrifices	Present Israel before the Lord for his favor	
Day of Atonement (Yom Kippur)	Lev 16; 23:26–32 Nu 29:7–11	7th month (Tishri) 10	Sept.-Oct.	A day of rest, fasting and sacrifices of atonement for priests and people and atonement for the tabernacle and altar	Cleanse priests and people from their sins and purify the Holy Place	Ro 3:24–26; Heb 9:7; 10:3, 19–22
Tabernacles (Booths) (Ingathering)	Ex 23:16b; 34:22b; Lev 23:33–36a, 39–43; Nu 29:12–34; Dt 16:13–15; Zec 14:16–19	7th month (Tishri) 15–21	Sept.-Oct.	A week of celebration for the harvest; living in booths and offering sacrifices	Memorialize the journey from Egypt to Canaan; give thanks for the productivity of Canaan	Jn 7:2,37
Sacred Assembly	Lev 23:36b; Nu 29:35–38	7th month (Tishri) 22	Sept.-Oct.	A day of convocation, rest and offering sacrifices	Commemorate the closing of the cycle of feasts	
Purim	Est 9:18–32	12th month (Adar) 14,15	Feb.-Mar.	A day of joy and feasting and giving presents	Remind the Israelites of their national deliverance in the time of Esther	

On Kislev 25 (mid-December) Hanukkah, the feast of dedication or festival of lights, commemorated the purification of the temple and altar in the Maccabean period (165/4 B.C.). This feast is mentioned in Jn 10:22.

Numbers

Books of the Law

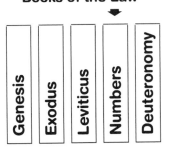

Purpose/Theme:

Named for the numbering of the people of Israel, this book records their forty years of wandering in the wilderness before entering the Promised Land.

Key Verse:

"Whenever the cloud lifted from above the Tent, the Israelites set out; wherever the cloud settled, the Israelites encamped" (9:17).

Main People:

Moses, Aaron, Joshua, Caleb, Miriam and the Priests

Outline:

The events in the book of Numbers took about 40 years.
☐ The preparation for the journey (Numbers 1—10)
☐ The wilderness wanderings (Numbers 10—20)
☐ The journey to Canaan (Numbers 21—36)

When Events Happened

◄ 1450 BC   1400 BC ►

JOSHUA, CALEB   MOSES, JOSHUA

Encampment of the Tribes of Israel

Numbers 2:1-31; 10:11-33

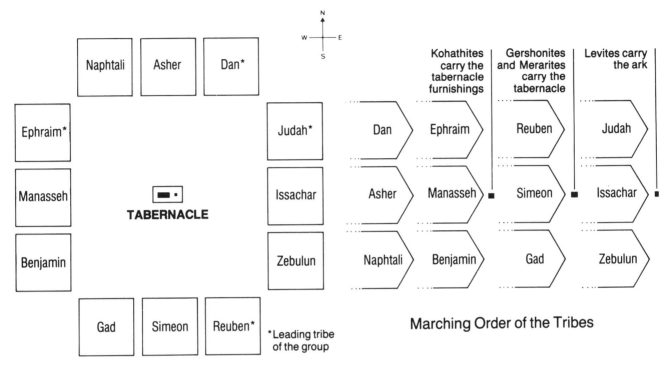

*Leading tribe
of the group

Marching Order of the Tribes

Cities of Refuge

Numbers 35:6-34; Joshua 20:1-9

The idea of providing cities of refuge (Jos 20:1-9) for capital offenses is rooted in the tension between customary tribal law (retaliation or revenge, in which the blood relative is obligated to execute vengeance) and civil law (carried out less personally by an assembly according to a standard code of justice).

Blood feuds are usually associated with nomadic groups; legal procedures, with villages and towns. Israel, a society in the process of sedentarization, found it necessary to adopt an intermediate step regulating manslaughter, so that an innocent person would not be killed before standing trial. Absolution was possible only by being cleared by his hometown assembly, and by the eventual death of the high priest, which freed the offender from ritual pollution.

The six cities of refuge are shown in bold type.

Deuteronomy

Books of the Law

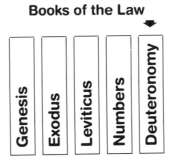

Genesis | Exodus | Leviticus | Numbers | Deuteronomy

Purpose/Theme:
The term "Deuteronomy" refers to the second stating of the Law of Moses. The book also rehearses some of the history of the Jews and records some of Moses' great speeches.

Key Verse:
"I have set before you life and death, blessings and curses. Now choose life, so that you and your children may live" (30:19).

Main People:
Moses, Joshua

Outline:
☐ Moses' First Speech to the People "Looking Back" (Deuteronomy 1—4)
☐ Moses' Second Speech to the People "Looking Up" (Deuteronomy 5—26)
☐ Moses' Third Speech to the People "Looking Out" (Deuteronomy 27—33)
☐ Moses' Death (Deuteronomy 34)

When Events Happened

1475 BC   1400 BC

MOSES

Major Social Concerns in the Covenant

1. Personhood
Everyone's person is to be secure (Ex 20:13; Dt 5:17; Ex 21:16-21,26-31; Lev 19:14; Dt 24:7; 27:18).

2. False Accusation
Everyone is to be secure against slander and false accusation (Ex 20:16; Dt 5:20; Ex 23:1-3; Lev 19:16; Dt 19:15-21).

3. Woman
No woman is to be taken advantage of within her subordinate status in society (Ex 21:7-11,20, 26-32; 22:16-17; Dt 21:10-14; 22:13-30; 24:1-5).

4. Punishment
Punishment for wrongdoing shall not be excessive so that the culprit is dehumanized (Dt 25:1-5).

5. Dignity
Every Israelite's dignity and right to be God's freedman and servant are to be honored and safeguarded (Ex 21:2,5-6; Lev 25; Dt 15:12-18).

6. Inheritance
Every Israelite's inheritance in the promised land is to be secure (Lev 25; Nu 27:5-7; 36:1-9; Dt 25:5-10).

7. Property
Everyone's property is to be secure (Ex 20:15; Dt 5:19; Ex 21:33-36; 22:1-15; 23:4-5; Lev 19:35-36; Dt 22:1-4; 25:13-15).

8. Fruit of Labor
Everyone is to receive the fruit of his labors (Lev 19:13; Dt 24:14; 25:4).

9. Fruit of the Ground
Everyone is to share the fruit of the ground (Ex 23:10-11; Lev 19:9-10; 23:22; 25:3-55; Dt 14:28-29; 24:19-21).

10. Rest on Sabbath
Everyone, down to the humblest servant and the resident alien, is to share in the weekly rest of God's Sabbath (Ex 20:8-11; Dt 5:12-15; Ex 23:12).

11. Marriage
The marriage relationship is to be kept inviolate (Ex 20:14; Dt 5:18; see also Lev 18:6-23; 20:10-21; Dt 22:13-30).

12. Exploitation
No one, however disabled, impoverished or powerless, is to be oppressed or exploited (Ex 22:21-27; Lev 19:14,33-34; 25:35-36; Dt 23:19; 24:6,12-15,17; 27:18).

13. Fair Trial
Everyone is to have free access to the courts and is to be afforded a fair trial (Ex 23:6,8; Lev 19:15; Dt 1:17; 10:17-18; 16:18-20; 17:8-13; 19:15-21).

14. Social Order
Every person's God-given place in the social order is to be honored (Ex 20:12; Dt 5:16; Ex 21:15,17; 22:28; Lev 19:3,32; 20:9; Dt 17:8-13; 21:15-21; 27:16).

15. Law
No one shall be above the law, not even the king (Dt 17:18-20).

16. Animals
Concern for the welfare of other creatures is to be extended to the animal world (Ex 23:5,11; Lev 25:7; Dt 22:4,6-7; 25:4).

Books of History

Joshua | Judges | Ruth | First Samuel | Second Samuel | First Kings | Second Kings | First Chronicles | Second Chronicles | Ezra | Nehemiah | Esther

God brought His nation to a new homeland. He helped them to defeat their enemies and picked out kings to rule them. Sometimes the people remembered God and His laws. More often they did just what they wanted and got into trouble. The nation divided itself in half. Both halves ended up being carried away by their enemies. Then the people had only God's promise to give them back their nation and to send the greatest King of all time.

When Events Happened

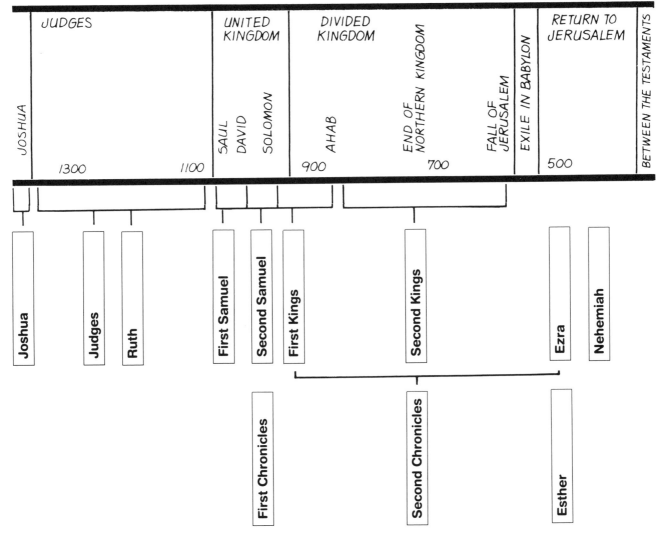

Joshua

The Books of History

Joshua | Judges | Ruth | First Samuel | Second Samuel | First Kings | Second Kings | First Chronicles | Second Chronicles | Ezra | Nehemiah | Esther

Purpose/Theme:

To record the Jewish conquest of the land of Canaan under Joshua, successor to Moses, and to describe the tribal boundaries in the new land.

Key Verse:

"Choose for yourselves this day whom you will serve . . . . But as for me and my household, we will serve the Lord" (24:15).

Main People:

Joshua, Rahab

Outline:

☐ The mobilization of the army (Joshua 1,2)
☐ The forward march (Joshua 3—5)
☐ The fall of Jericho (Joshua 6)
☐ The campaign at Ai (Joshua 7,8)
☐ The southern campaign (Joshua 9)

☐ The central campaign (Joshua 10)
☐ The northern campaign (Joshua 11)
☐ The defeated kings (Joshua 12)
☐ The division of the land (Joshua 13—22)
☐ Joshua's farewell and death (Joshua 23,24)

When Events Happened

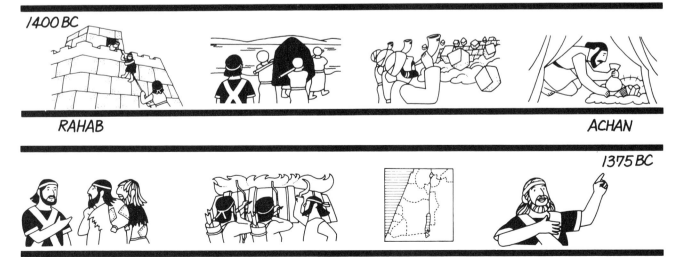

1400 BC

RAHAB   ACHAN

1375 BC

JOSHUA

Conquest of Canaan

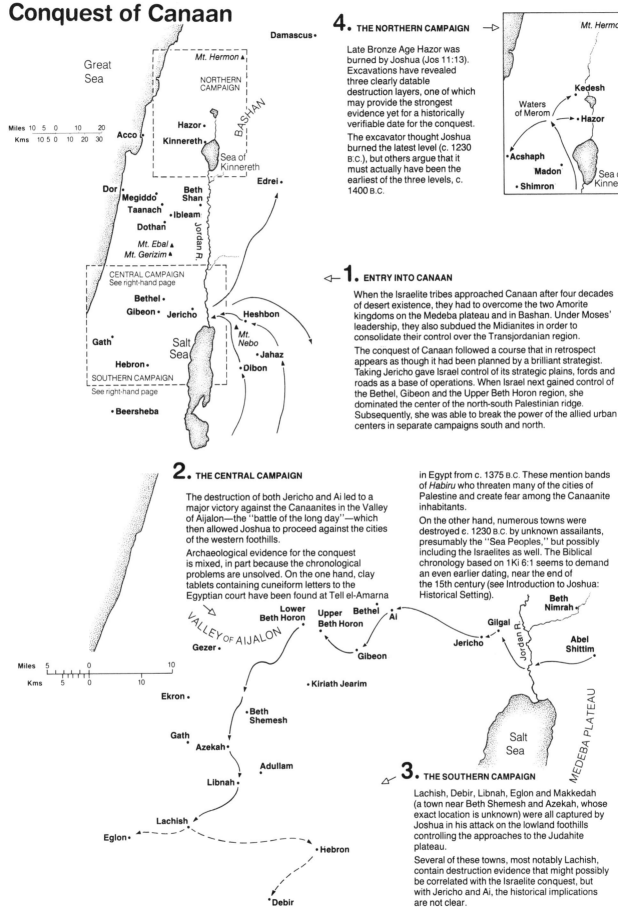

4. THE NORTHERN CAMPAIGN

Late Bronze Age Hazor was burned by Joshua (Jos 11:13). Excavations have revealed three clearly datable destruction layers, one of which may provide the strongest evidence yet for a historically verifiable date for the conquest.

The excavator thought Joshua burned the latest level (c. 1230 B.C.), but others argue that it must actually have been the earliest of the three levels, c. 1400 B.C.

1. ENTRY INTO CANAAN

When the Israelite tribes approached Canaan after four decades of desert existence, they had to overcome the two Amorite kingdoms on the Medeba plateau and in Bashan. Under Moses' leadership, they also subdued the Midianites in order to consolidate their control over the Transjordanian region.

The conquest of Canaan followed a course that in retrospect appears as though it had been planned by a brilliant strategist. Taking Jericho gave Israel control of its strategic plains, fords and roads as a base of operations. When Israel next gained control of the Bethel, Gibeon and the Upper Beth Horon region, she dominated the center of the north-south Palestinian ridge. Subsequently, she was able to break the power of the allied urban centers in separate campaigns south and north.

2. THE CENTRAL CAMPAIGN

The destruction of both Jericho and Ai led to a major victory against the Canaanites in the Valley of Aijalon—the "battle of the long day"—which then allowed Joshua to proceed against the cities of the western foothills.

Archaeological evidence for the conquest is mixed, in part because the chronological problems are unsolved. On the one hand, clay tablets containing cuneiform letters to the Egyptian court have been found at Tell el-Amarna in Egypt from c. 1375 B.C. These mention bands of *Habiru* who threaten many of the cities of Palestine and create fear among the Canaanite inhabitants.

On the other hand, numerous towns were destroyed c. 1230 B.C. by unknown assailants, presumably the "Sea Peoples," but possibly including the Israelites as well. The Biblical chronology based on 1 Ki 6:1 seems to demand an even earlier dating, near the end of the 15th century (see Introduction to Joshua: Historical Setting).

3. THE SOUTHERN CAMPAIGN

Lachish, Debir, Libnah, Eglon and Makkedah (a town near Beth Shemesh and Azekah, whose exact location is unknown) were all captured by Joshua in his attack on the lowland foothills controlling the approaches to the Judahite plateau.

Several of these towns, most notably Lachish, contain destruction evidence that might possibly be correlated with the Israelite conquest, but with Jericho and Ai, the historical implications are not clear.

Judges
The Books of History

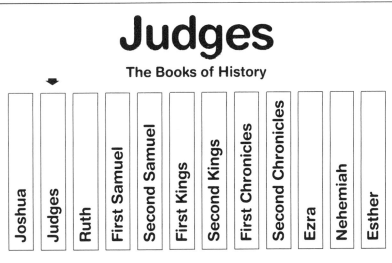

Joshua | Judges | Ruth | First Samuel | Second Samuel | First Kings | Second Kings | First Chronicles | Second Chronicles | Ezra | Nehemiah | Esther

Purpose/Theme:
After arriving in Canaan, many Jews became disobedient to God. The book of Judges shows how God raised up leaders to call them back to faithfulness and to continue the conquest of the land.

Key Verses:
"Whenever the Lord raised up a judge for them, he was with the judge and saved them out of the hands of their enemies . . . . But when the judge died, the people returned to ways even more corrupt than those of their fathers" (2:18-19).

Main People:
The judges. The chief judges were Deborah, Gideon, Samson and (in the book of 1 Samuel) Samuel.

Outline:
☐ The Israelites did not possess all the land (Judges 1,2)
☐ God sent judges (Judges 3—16)
- Othniel and Ehud (Judges 3)
- Deborah (Judges 4,5)
- Gideon (Judges 6-8)
- The wickedness of Abimelech (Judges 9)
- Jephthah (Judges 10—12)
- Samson (Judges 13-16)

☐ The Israelites did not keep God's laws (Judges 17—21)

When Events Happened

1375 BC

OTHNIEL   DEBORAH

1050 BC

GIDEON   JEPHTHAH   SAMSON

Five Cities of the Philistines

Like a string of opulent pearls along the Mediterranean coast, the five cities of the Philistines comprise a litany of familiar Biblical names: Gaza, Ashkelon, Ashdod, Ekron and Gath.

Each was a commercial emporium with important connections reaching as far as Egypt along the coastal route, the "interstate highway" of the ancient world. The ships of Phoenicia, Cyprus, Crete and the Aegean called at Philistia's seaports, which included a site today called Tell Qasile, where a Philistine temple has been found, on the Yarkon River just north of modern Tel Aviv.

The Philistine plain itself was an arid, loess-covered lowland bordering on the desert to the south—a stretch of undulating sand dunes adjacent to the sea—and the foothills of the Judahite plateau on the east. No area in Biblical history was more frequently contested than the western foothills (the Shephelah region), lying on the border between Judea and Philistia. Beth Shemesh, Timnah, Azekah and Ziklag were among the towns coveted by both Israelites and Philistines, and they figure in the stories of Samson, Goliath and David.

The area to the north of Philistia, the plain of Sharon, was also contested at various periods: During Saul's reign the Philistines even held Beth Shan and the Esdraelon valley. Later, from about the time of Baasha on, a long border war was conducted by the Israelites at Gibbethon. Originally a part of Judah's tribal allotment, the coastal area was never totally wrested away from the Philistines who may have begun their occupation as early as the time of Abraham.

Gideon's Battles

The story of Gideon begins with a graphic portrayal of one of the most striking facts of life in the Fertile Crescent: the periodic migration of nomadic people from the Aramean desert into the settled areas of Palestine. Each spring the tents of the *bedouin* herdsmen appear overnight almost as if by magic, scattered on the hills and fields of the farming districts. Conflict between these two ways of life (herdsmen and farmers) was inevitable.

In the Biblical period, the vast numbers and warlike practice of the herdsmen reduced the village people to near vassalage. Gideon's answer was twofold: (1) religious reform, starting with his own family; and (2) military action, based on a coalition of northern Israelite tribes. The location of Gideon's hometown, "Ophrah of the Abiezrites," is not known with certainty, but probably was ancient Aper (modern Afula) in the Valley of Jezreel.

The battle at the spring of Harod is justly celebrated for its strategic brilliance. Denied the use of the only local water source, the Midianites camped in the valley and fell victim to the small band of Israelites, who attacked them from the heights of the hill of Moreh.

The main battle took place north of the hill near the village of Endor at the foot of Mount Tabor. Fleeing by way of the Jordan Valley, the Midianites were trapped when the Ephraimites seized the fords of the Jordan from below Beth Shan to Beth Barah near Adam.

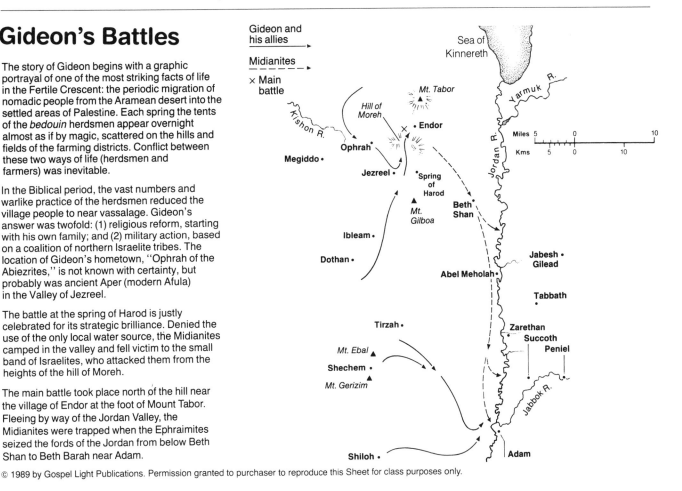

Ruth
The Books of History

Joshua | Judges | Ruth | First Samuel | Second Samuel | First Kings | Second Kings | First Chronicles | Second Chronicles | Ezra | Nehemiah | Esther

Purpose/Theme:
This book was written to show that King David, the forerunner of the Messiah, was a descendant of Ruth, a Moabite (non-Jewish) woman—and thus that God is with those who follow him.

Key Verse:
"Don't urge me to leave you or to turn back from you. Where you go I will go, and where you stay I will stay. Your people will be my people and your God my God" (1:16).

Main People:
Ruth, Naomi, Boaz

Outline:
☐ Ruth's husband, Mahlon, an Israelite, died in Moab (Ruth 1).
☐ Ruth decided to go to Israel with Mahlon's mother, Naomi (Ruth 1:1-18).
☐ Ruth cared for Naomi (Ruth 1:19—2:23).
☐ Ruth wanted to be with Boaz (Ruth 3:1-18).
☐ Ruth married Boaz and had a son (Ruth 4:1-22).

When Events Happened

1375 BC   RUTH, NAOMI   BOAZ   1050 BC

The Book of Ruth

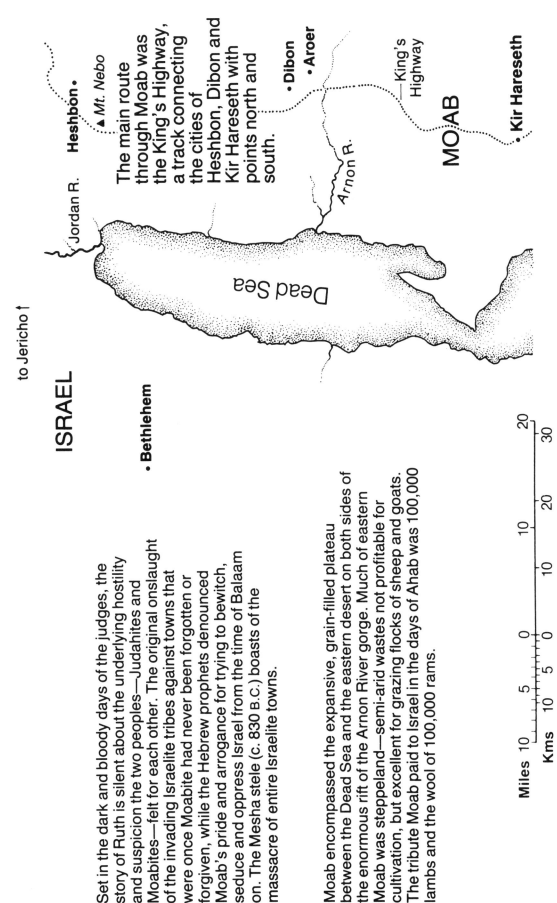

to Jericho ↑

ISRAEL

• Bethlehem

Jordan R.

Heshbon •

▲ Mt. Nebo

The main route through Moab was the King's Highway, a track connecting the cities of Heshbon, Dibon and Kir Hareseth with points north and south.

• Dibon

• Aroer

Arnon R.

Dead Sea

— King's Highway

MOAB

• Kir Hareseth

Set in the dark and bloody days of the judges, the story of Ruth is silent about the underlying hostility and suspicion the two peoples—Judahites and Moabites—felt for each other. The original onslaught of the invading Israelite tribes against towns that were once Moabite had never been forgotten or forgiven, while the Hebrew prophets denounced Moab's pride and arrogance for trying to bewitch, seduce and oppress Israel from the time of Balaam on. The Mesha stele (c. 830 B.C.) boasts of the massacre of entire Israelite towns.

Moab encompassed the expansive, grain-filled plateau between the Dead Sea and the eastern desert on both sides of the enormous rift of the Arnon River gorge. Much of eastern Moab was steppeland—semi-arid wastes not profitable for cultivation, but excellent for grazing flocks of sheep and goats. The tribute Moab paid to Israel in the days of Ahab was 100,000 lambs and the wool of 100,000 rams.

Miles 10   5   0   10   20

Kms 10   5   0   10   20   30

1 Samuel
The Books of History

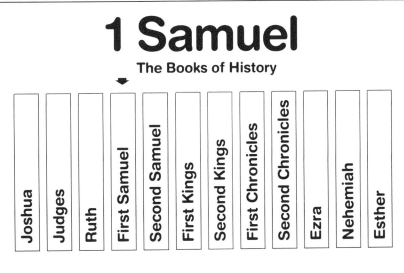

| Joshua | Judges | Ruth | First Samuel | Second Samuel | First Kings | Second Kings | First Chronicles | Second Chronicles | Ezra | Nehemiah | Esther |

Purpose/Theme:
To record the history of Israel from the birth of Samuel, the last judge, to the death of Saul, the first king, and the anointing of his successor, David.

Key Verses:
"We want a king over us. Then we will be like all the other nations, with a king to lead us and to go out before us and fight our battles" (8:19-20).

Main People:
Eli, Samuel, Saul, David

Outline:
☐ Samuel—The last of the judges (1 Samuel 1—8)
☐ Saul—Israel's first king (1 Samuel 9—15)
☐ David—A new king chosen (1 Samuel 16—31)

When Events Happened

1100 BC   1050 BC

ELI, SAMUEL   SAMUEL   SAUL   DAVID

1010 BC

SAUL'S DEATH

David's Family Tree

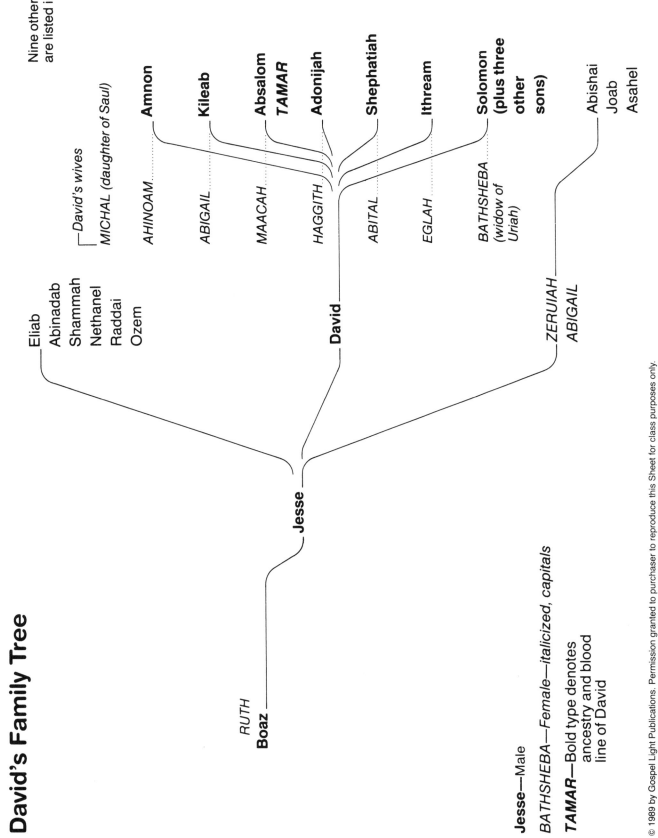

Nine other sons of David are listed in 1 Ch 3:6-8.

David's wives

MICHAL (daughter of Saul)

AHINOAM — Amnon

ABIGAIL — Kileab

MAACAH — Absalom, TAMAR

HAGGITH — Adonijah

ABITAL — Shephatiah

EGLAH — Ithream

BATHSHEBA (widow of Uriah) — Solomon (plus three other sons)

Eliab
Abinadab
Shammah
Nethanel
Raddai
Ozem

David

ZERUIAH — Abishai, Joab, Asahel
ABIGAIL

Jesse

RUTH
Boaz

Jesse—Male

BATHSHEBA—Female—italicized, capitals

TAMAR—Bold type denotes ancestry and blood line of David

Exploits of David

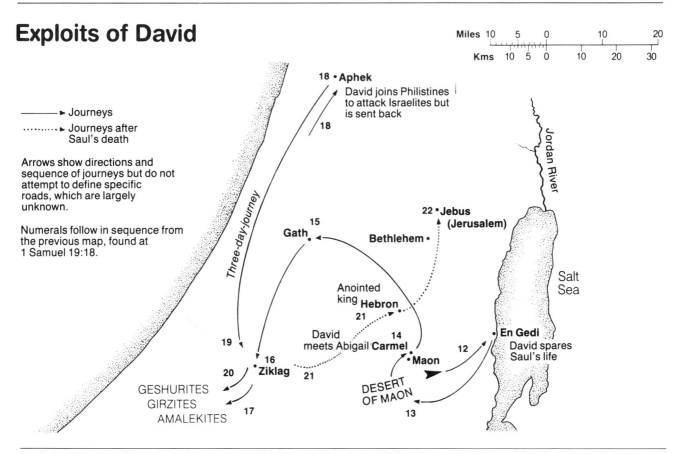

Miles 10 5 0 10 20
Kms 10 5 0 10 20 30

——▶ Journeys

·········▶ Journeys after Saul's death

Arrows show directions and sequence of journeys but do not attempt to define specific roads, which are largely unknown.

Numerals follow in sequence from the previous map, found at 1 Samuel 19:18.

18 • Aphek
David joins Philistines to attack Israelites but is sent back
18

Jordan River

Three-day-journey

22 • Jebus (Jerusalem)

15
Gath •   Bethlehem •

Salt Sea

Anointed king Hebron
21

En Gedi
David spares Saul's life

19
David meets Abigail Carmel 14
12

16
Ziklag
20   21   • Maon

DESERT OF MAON

GESHURITES
GIRZITES
AMALEKITES   17

13

David the Fugitive

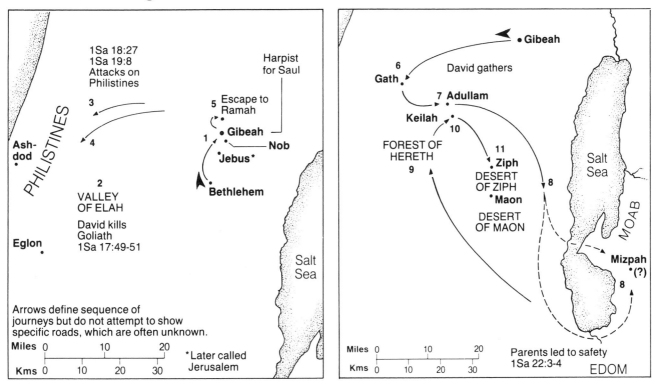

1Sa 18:27
1Sa 19:8
Attacks on Philistines

Harpist for Saul

3

5 Escape to Ramah

PHILISTINES

Ash-dod •

4

1   • Gibeah

Nob

Jebus *

2
VALLEY OF ELAH

David kills Goliath
1Sa 17:49-51

Bethlehem

Eglon •

Salt Sea

Arrows define sequence of journeys but do not attempt to show specific roads, which are often unknown.

Miles 0   10   20
Kms 0   10   20   30

*Later called Jerusalem

• Gibeah

David gathers

6
Gath •

7 Adullam

Keilah
10

FOREST OF HERETH
9

11
• Ziph

DESERT OF ZIPH
• Maon

DESERT OF MAON

Salt Sea

MOAB

8

Mizpah • (?)

8

Miles 0   10   20
Kms 0   10   20   30

Parents led to safety
1Sa 22:3-4

EDOM

2 Samuel
The Books of History

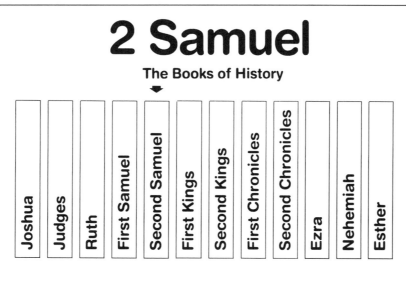

| Joshua | Judges | Ruth | First Samuel | Second Samuel | First Kings | Second Kings | First Chronicles | Second Chronicles | Ezra | Nehemiah | Esther |

Purpose/Theme:
To record the history of Israel under King David, whom God called to be the beginning of an eternal dynasty that eventually included the Messiah.

Key Verse:
"When your days are over and you rest with your fathers, I will raise up your offspring to succeed you, who will come from your own body, and I will establish his kingdom. He is the one who will build a house for my Name, and I will establish the throne of his kingdom forever" (7:12-13).

Main People:
David, Ish-bosheth, Abner, Mephibosheth, Uriah, Bathsheba, Nathan, Joab, Amnon, Absalom

Outline:
☐ David's rise—king and ruler (2 Samuel 1—10)
☐ David's fall—sin and problems (2 Samuel 11—20)
☐ David's last days—troubles in David's family and kingdom (2 Samuel 21—24)

When Events Happened

1010 BC

DAVID   NATHAN   MEPHIBOSHETH

970 BC

BATHSHEBA

1. The City of the Jebusites and
2. David's Jerusalem

Substantial historical evidence, both Biblical and extra-Biblical, places the temple of Herod (and before it the temples of Zerubbabel and of Solomon) on the holy spot where King David built an altar to the Lord. David had purchased the land from Araunah the Jebusite, who was using the exposed

bedrock as a threshing floor (2Sa 24:18-25). Tradition claims a much older sanctity for the site, associating it with the altar of Abraham on Mount Moriah (Ge 22:1-19). The writer of Genesis equates Moriah with "the Mountain of the LORD," and other OT shrines originated in altars erected by Abraham.

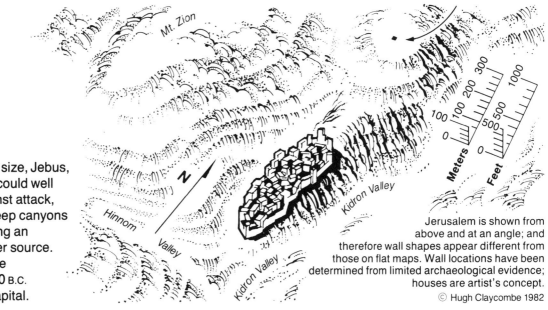

c. 1000 B.C.

Barely 12 acres in size, Jebus, a Canaanite city, could well defend itself against attack, with walls atop steep canyons and shafts reaching an underground water source. David captured the stronghold, c. 1000 B.C. and made it his capital.

Jerusalem is shown from above and at an angle; and therefore wall shapes appear different from those on flat maps. Wall locations have been determined from limited archaeological evidence; houses are artist's concept.

© Hugh Claycombe 1982

For further reference to the development of Jerusalem see: page 73, *Solomon's Jerusalem;* page 99, *Jerusalem of the Returning Exiles;* page 139, *Jerusalem During the Time of the Prophets.*

---

2 Samuel 5:6-10

David Conquers Jerusalem

The king and his men marched to Jerusalem to attack the Jebusites, who lived there. The Jebusites said to David, "You will not get in here; even the blind and the lame can ward you off." They thought, "David cannot get in here." Nevertheless, David captured the fortress of Zion, the City of David.

On that day, David said, "Anyone who conquers the Jebusites will have to use the water shaft to

reach those lame and blind who are David's enemies." That is why they say, "The 'blind and lame' will not enter the palace."

David then took up residence in the fortress and called it the City of David. He built up the area around it, from the supporting terraces inward. And he became more and more powerful, because the LORD God Almighty was with him.

David's Conquests

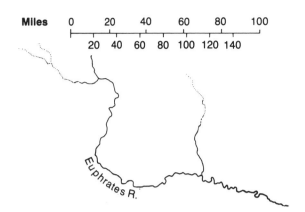

Miles

Once he had become king over all Israel (2Sa 5:1-5), David:

1. Conquered the Jebusite citadel of Zion/Jerusalem and made it his royal city (2Sa 5:6-10);

2. Received the recognition of and assurance of friendship from Hiram of Tyre, king of the Phoenicians (2Sa 5:11-12);

3. Decisively defeated the Philistines so that their hold on Israelite territory was broken and their threat to Israel eliminated (2Sa 5:17-25; 8:1);

4. Defeated the Moabites and imposed his authority over them (2Sa 8:2);

5. Crushed the Aramean kingdoms of Hadadezer (king of Zobah), Damascus and Maacah and put them under tribute (2Sa 8:3-8; 10:6-19). Talmai, the Aramean king of Geshur, apparently had made peace with David while he was still reigning in Hebron and sealed the alliance by giving his daughter in marriage to David (2Sa 3:3; see 1Ch 2:23);

6. Subdued Edom and incorporated it into his empire (2Sa 8:13-14);

7. Defeated the Ammonites and brought them into subjection (2Sa 12:19-31);

8. Subjugated the remaining Canaanite cities that had previously maintained their independence from and hostility toward Israel, such as Beth Shan, Megiddo, Taanach and Dor.

Since David had earlier crushed the Amalekites (1Sa 30:17), his wars thus completed the conquest begun by Joshua and secured all the borders of Israel. His empire (united Israel plus the subjugated kingdoms) reached from Ezion Geber on the eastern arm of the Red Sea to the Euphrates River.

1 Kings
The Books of History

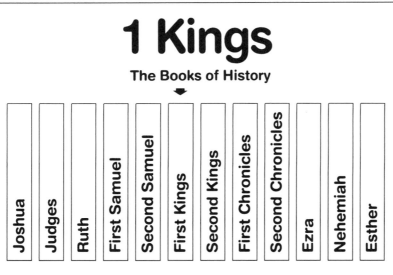

Joshua | Judges | Ruth | First Samuel | Second Samuel | First Kings | Second Kings | First Chronicles | Second Chronicles | Ezra | Nehemiah | Esther

Purpose/Theme:
First Kings records the glory of the Jewish nation under King Solomon, and the tragic split of the kingdom into Israel in the north, and Judah in the south. It is at this time that we also see the rise of the prophets as a powerful religious force.

Key Verses:
"Be strong, show yourself a man, and observe what the Lord your God requires: Walk in his ways, and keep his decrees and commands, his laws and requirements . . . so that you may prosper in all you do and wherever you go" (2:2-3).

Main People:
David, Solomon, Rehoboam, Nathan, Jeroboam, Ahab, Jezebel, Elijah, Elisha

Outline:
☐ The reign of Solomon (1 Kings 1—10)
☐ The death of Solomon and division of the kingdom (1 Kings 11—16)
☐ King Ahab and his wife Jezebel introduce Baal worship (1 Kings 16)
☐ The prophet Elijah defeats the prophets of Baal (1 Kings 17,18)
☐ Ahab does evil (1 Kings 19—22)

When Events Happened

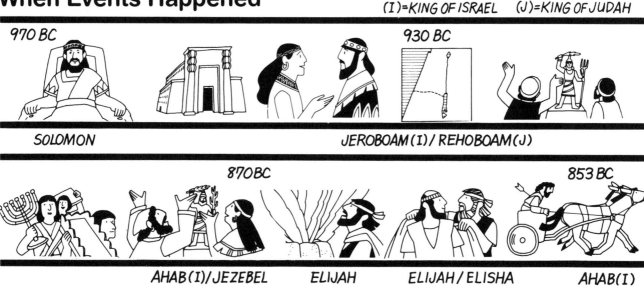

(I)=KING OF ISRAEL   (J)=KING OF JUDAH

970 BC   930 BC

SOLOMON   JEROBOAM(I) / REHOBOAM(J)

870 BC   853 BC

AHAB(I)/JEZEBEL   ELIJAH   ELIJAH/ELISHA   AHAB(I)

Solomon's Temple

960-586 B.C.

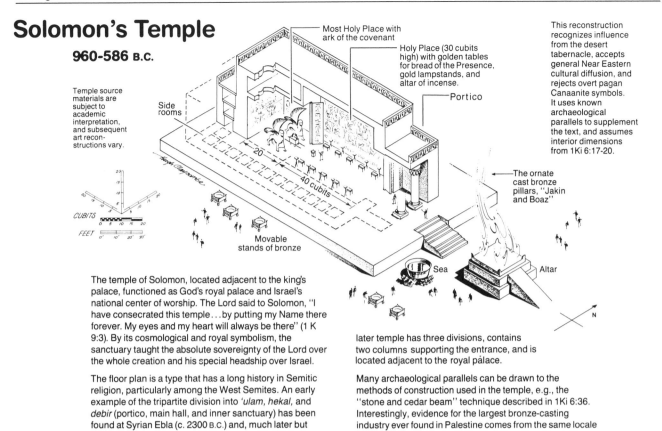

Temple source materials are subject to academic interpretation, and subsequent art reconstructions vary.

Most Holy Place with ark of the covenant

Holy Place (30 cubits high) with golden tables for bread of the Presence, gold lampstands, and altar of incense.

Portico

This reconstruction recognizes influence from the desert tabernacle, accepts general Near Eastern cultural diffusion, and rejects overt pagan Canaanite symbols. It uses known archaeological parallels to supplement the text, and assumes interior dimensions from 1Ki 6:17-20.

Side rooms

The ornate cast bronze pillars, "Jakin and Boaz"

Movable stands of bronze

Sea

Altar

CUBITS

FEET

N

The temple of Solomon, located adjacent to the king's palace, functioned as God's royal palace and Israel's national center of worship. The Lord said to Solomon, "I have consecrated this temple...by putting my Name there forever. My eyes and my heart will always be there" (1 K 9:3). By its cosmological and royal symbolism, the sanctuary taught the absolute sovereignty of the Lord over the whole creation and his special headship over Israel.

The floor plan is a type that has a long history in Semitic religion, particularly among the West Semites. An early example of the tripartite division into *'ulam, hekal,* and *debir* (portico, main hall, and inner sanctuary) has been found at Syrian Ebla (c. 2300 B.C.) and, much later but more contemporaneous with Solomon, at Tell Tainat in the Orontes basin (c. 900 B.C.). Like Solomon's, the

later temple has three divisions, contains two columns supporting the entrance, and is located adjacent to the royal palace.

Many archaeological parallels can be drawn to the methods of construction used in the temple, e.g., the "stone and cedar beam" technique described in 1Ki 6:36. Interestingly, evidence for the largest bronze-casting industry ever found in Palestine comes from the same locale and period as that indicated in Scripture: Zarethan in the Jordan Valley c. 1000 B.C.

© Hugh Claycombe 1986

Temple Furnishings

Glimpses of the rich ornamentation of Solomon's temple can be gained through recent discoveries that illumine the text of 1 Ki 6-7.

1 Kings 7:13-51

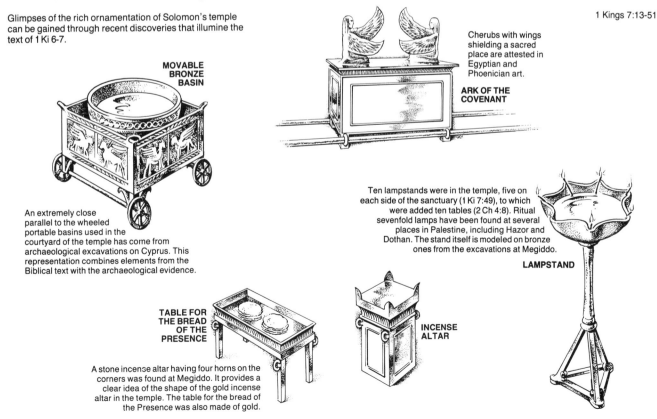

MOVABLE BRONZE BASIN

Cherubs with wings shielding a sacred place are attested in Egyptian and Phoenician art.

ARK OF THE COVENANT

An extremely close parallel to the wheeled portable basins used in the courtyard of the temple has come from archaeological excavations on Cyprus. This representation combines elements from the Biblical text with the archaeological evidence.

Ten lampstands were in the temple, five on each side of the sanctuary (1 Ki 7:49), to which were added ten tables (2 Ch 4:8). Ritual sevenfold lamps have been found at several places in Palestine, including Hazor and Dothan. The stand itself is modeled on bronze ones from the excavations at Megiddo.

LAMPSTAND

TABLE FOR THE BREAD OF THE PRESENCE

INCENSE ALTAR

A stone incense altar having four horns on the corners was found at Megiddo. It provides a clear idea of the shape of the gold incense altar in the temple. The table for the bread of the Presence was also made of gold.

Rulers of Israel and Judah

DATA AND DATES IN
ORDER OF SEQUENCE

No.	Scripture	Ruler	Synchronism	Notes	Years	Dates (B.C.)
1.	1Ki 12:1-24; 14:21-31	*Rehoboam (Judah)*			17 years	930-913
2.	1Ki 12:25—14:20	Jeroboam I (Israel)			22 years	930-909
3.	1Ki 15:1-8	*Abijah (Judah)*	18th of Jeroboam		3 years	913-910
4.	1Ki 15:9-24	*Asa (Judah)*	20th of Jeroboam		41 years	910-869
5.	1Ki 15:25-31	Nadab (Israel)	2nd of Asa		2 years	909-908
6.	1Ki 15:32—16:7	Baasha (Israel)	3rd of Asa		24 years	908-886
7.	1Ki 16:8-14	Elah (Israel)	26th of Asa		2 years	886-885
8.	1Ki 16:15-20	Zimri (Israel)	27th of Asa		7 days	885
9.	1Ki 16:21-22	Tibni (Israel)		Overlap with Omri		885-880
10.	1Ki 16:23-28	Omri (Israel)	27th of Asa; 31st of Asa	Made king by the people; Overlap with Tibni; Beginning of sole reign; Official reign = 11 actual years	12 years	885; 885-880; 880
11.	1Ki 16:29—22:40	Ahab (Israel)	38th of Asa	Official reign = 21 actual years	22 years	874-853
12.	1Ki 22:41-50	*Jehoshaphat (Judah)*	4th of Ahab	Co-regency with Asa; Official reign; Beginning of sole reign; Has Jehoram as regent	25 years	872-869; 872-848; 869; 853-848
13.	1Ki 22:51—2Ki 1:18	Ahaziah (Israel)	17th of Jehoshaphat	Official reign = 1 yr. actual reign	2 years	853-852
14.	2Ki 1:17; 2Ki 3:1—8:15	Joram (Israel)	2nd of Jehoram; 18th of Jehoshaphat	Official reign = 11 actual years	12 years	852-841
15.	2Ki 8:16-24	*Jehoram (Judah)*	5th of Joram	Beginning of sole reign; Official reign = 7 actual years	8 years	848; 848-841
16.	2Ki 8:25-29; 9:29	*Ahaziah (Judah)*	12th of Joram; 11th of Joram	Nonaccession-year reckoning; Accession-year reckoning	1 year	841; 841
17.	2Ki 9:30—10:36	Jehu (Israel)			28 years	841-814
18.	2Ki 11	*Athaliah (Judah)*			7 years	841-835
19.	2Ki 12	*Joash (Judah)*	7th of Jehu		40 years	835-796
20.	2Ki 13:1-9	Jehoahaz (Israel)	23rd of Joash		17 years	814-798
21.	2Ki 13:10-25	Jehoash (Israel)	37th of Joash		16 years	798-782
22.	2Ki 14:1-22	**Amaziah (Judah)**	2nd of Jehoash	Overlap with Azariah	29 years	**796-767; 792-767**
23.	2Ki 14:23-29	**Jeroboam II (Israel)**	15th of Amaziah	Co-regency with Jehoash; Total reign; Beginning of sole reign	41 years	**793-782; 793-753**; 782
24.	2Ki 15:1-7	**Azariah (Judah)**	27th of Jeroboam	Overlap with Amaziah; Total reign; Beginning of sole reign	52 years	**792-767; 792-740**; 767
25.	2Ki 15:8-12	**Zechariah (Israel)**	38th of Azariah		6 months	**753**
26.	2Ki 15:13-15	**Shallum (Israel)**	39th of Azariah		1 month	**752**
27.	2Ki 15:16-22	**Menahem (Israel)**	39th of Azariah	Ruled in Samaria	10 years	**752-742**
28.	2Ki 15:23-26	**Pekahiah (Israel)**	50th of Azariah		2 years	**742-740**
29.	2Ki 15:27-31	**Pekah (Israel)**	52nd of Azariah	In Gilead; overlapping years; Total reign; Beginning of sole reign	20 years	752-740; **752-732**; 740
30.	2Ki 15:32-38; 2Ki 15:30	**Jotham (Judah)**	2nd of Pekah	Co-regency with Azariah; Official reign; Reign to his 20th year; Beginning of co-regency; Total reign	16 years	**750-740; 750-735; 750-732**; 750; 735-715; 735
31.	2Ki 16	**Ahaz (Judah)**	17th of Pekah	From 20th of Jotham	16 years	**732-715**; 732
32.	2Ki 15:30; 2Ki 17	**Hoshea (Israel)**	12th of Ahaz*	20th of Jotham	9 years	**732-722**; 852
33.	2Ki 18:1—20:21	**Hezekiah (Judah)**	3rd of Hoshea*	Total reign	29 years	848; **715-686**
34.	2Ki 21:1-18	**Manasseh (Judah)**		Co-regency with Hezekiah; Total reign	55 years	848-841; **697-686; 697-642**
35.	2Ki 21:19-26	**Amon (Judah)**			2 years	841; **642-640**
36.	2Ki 22:1—23:30	**Josiah (Judah)**			31 years	**640-609**
37.	2Ki 23:31-33	**Jehoahaz (Judah)**			3 months	**609**
38.	2Ki 23:34—24:7	**Jehoiakim (Judah)**			11 years	**609-598**
39.	2Ki 24:8-17	**Jehoiachin (Judah)**			3 months	**598-597**
40.	2Ki 24:18—25:26	**Zedekiah (Judah)**			11 years	**597-586**

*These data arise when the reign of Hoshea is thrown 12 years in advance of its historical position.

Italics denote kings of Judah.
Non-italic type denotes kings of **Israel**.

Adapted from: *A Chronology of the Hebrew Kings* by Edwin R. Thiele.
© 1977 by The Zondervan Corporation. Used by permission.

Solomon's Jerusalem

950 B.C.

Solomon extended the city
northward from the original
site and there built his
magnificent temple.

His royal residence was
nearby; however, its
architecture and location
are unknown.

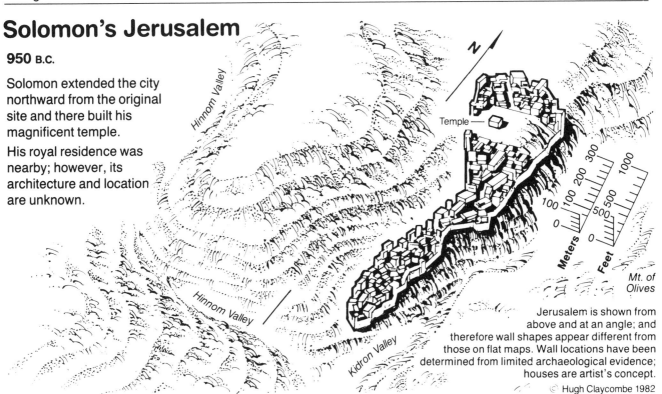

Jerusalem is shown from
above and at an angle; and
therefore wall shapes appear different from
those on flat maps. Wall locations have been
determined from limited archaeological evidence;
houses are artist's concept.

© Hugh Claycombe 1982

For further reference to the development of Jerusalem see: page 63, *The City of the Jebusites and David's Jerusalem;* page 99, *Jerusalem of the Returning Exiles;* page 139, *Jerusalem During the Time of the Prophets.*

Elijah

Elisha

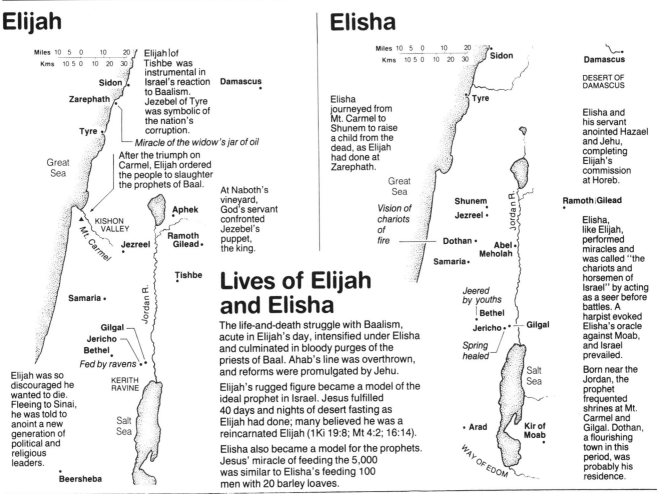

Elijah of
Tishbe was
instrumental in
Israel's reaction
to Baalism.
Jezebel of Tyre
was symbolic of
the nation's
corruption.

— *Miracle of the widow's jar of oil*

After the triumph on
Carmel, Elijah ordered
the people to slaughter
the prophets of Baal.

At Naboth's
vineyard,
God's servant
confronted
Jezebel's
puppet,
the king.

Elijah was so
discouraged he
wanted to die.
Fleeing to Sinai,
he was told to
anoint a new
generation of
political and
religious
leaders.

Elisha
journeyed from
Mt. Carmel to
Shunem to raise
a child from the
dead, as Elijah
had done at
Zarephath.

*Vision of
chariots
of
fire*

*Jeered
by youths*

*Spring
healed*

DESERT OF
DAMASCUS

Elisha and
his servant
anointed Hazael
and Jehu,
completing
Elijah's
commission
at Horeb.

Elisha,
like Elijah,
performed
miracles and
was called "the
chariots and
horsemen of
Israel" by acting
as a seer before
battles. A
harpist evoked
Elisha's oracle
against Moab,
and Israel
prevailed.

Born near the
Jordan, the
prophet
frequented
shrines at Mt.
Carmel and
Gilgal. Dothan,
a flourishing
town in this
period, was
probably his
residence.

Lives of Elijah and Elisha

The life-and-death struggle with Baalism,
acute in Elijah's day, intensified under Elisha
and culminated in bloody purges of the
priests of Baal. Ahab's line was overthrown,
and reforms were promulgated by Jehu.

Elijah's rugged figure became a model of the
ideal prophet in Israel. Jesus fulfilled
40 days and nights of desert fasting as
Elijah had done; many believed he was a
reincarnated Elijah (1Ki 19:8; Mt 4:2; 16:14).

Elisha also became a model for the prophets.
Jesus' miracle of feeding the 5,000
was similar to Elisha's feeding 100
men with 20 barley loaves.

The Divided Kingdom

930-586 B.C.

The division of Solomon's kingdom had geographical and political causes, with roots reaching back to earlier tribal rivalries. Israel was closer to Phoenician cities and major trade routes than Judah, whose heartland was a plateau-like ridge higher than the district around Samaria.

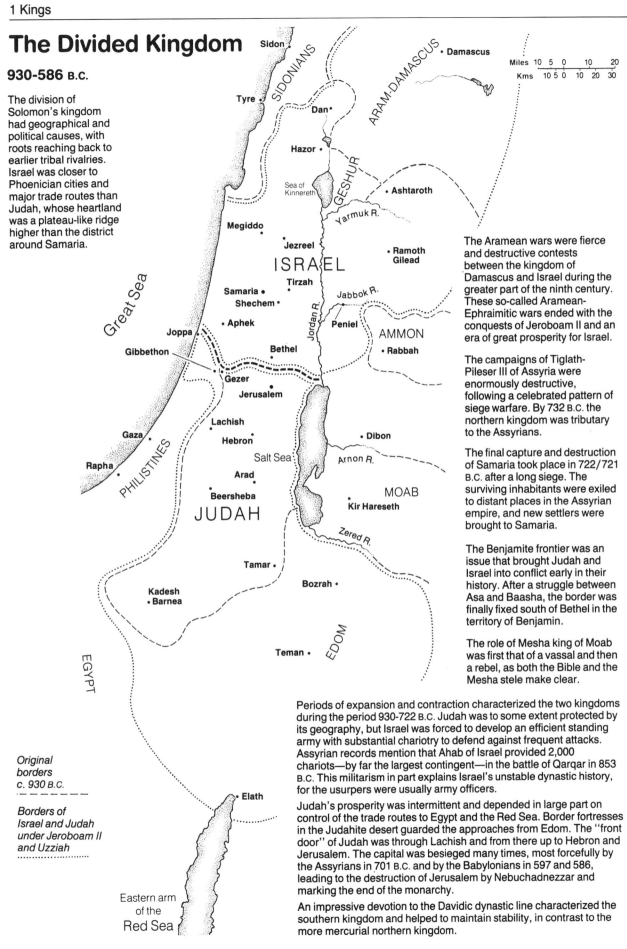

The Aramean wars were fierce and destructive contests between the kingdom of Damascus and Israel during the greater part of the ninth century. These so-called Aramean-Ephraimitic wars ended with the conquests of Jeroboam II and an era of great prosperity for Israel.

The campaigns of Tiglath-Pileser III of Assyria were enormously destructive, following a celebrated pattern of siege warfare. By 732 B.C. the northern kingdom was tributary to the Assyrians.

The final capture and destruction of Samaria took place in 722/721 B.C. after a long siege. The surviving inhabitants were exiled to distant places in the Assyrian empire, and new settlers were brought to Samaria.

The Benjamite frontier was an issue that brought Judah and Israel into conflict early in their history. After a struggle between Asa and Baasha, the border was finally fixed south of Bethel in the territory of Benjamin.

The role of Mesha king of Moab was first that of a vassal and then a rebel, as both the Bible and the Mesha stele make clear.

Periods of expansion and contraction characterized the two kingdoms during the period 930-722 B.C. Judah was to some extent protected by its geography, but Israel was forced to develop an efficient standing army with substantial chariotry to defend against frequent attacks. Assyrian records mention that Ahab of Israel provided 2,000 chariots—by far the largest contingent—in the battle of Qarqar in 853 B.C. This militarism in part explains Israel's unstable dynastic history, for the usurpers were usually army officers.

Judah's prosperity was intermittent and depended in large part on control of the trade routes to Egypt and the Red Sea. Border fortresses in the Judahite desert guarded the approaches from Edom. The "front door" of Judah was through Lachish and from there up to Hebron and Jerusalem. The capital was besieged many times, most forcefully by the Assyrians in 701 B.C. and by the Babylonians in 597 and 586, leading to the destruction of Jerusalem by Nebuchadnezzar and marking the end of the monarchy.

An impressive devotion to the Davidic dynastic line characterized the southern kingdom and helped to maintain stability, in contrast to the more mercurial northern kingdom.

2 Kings
The Books of History
▼

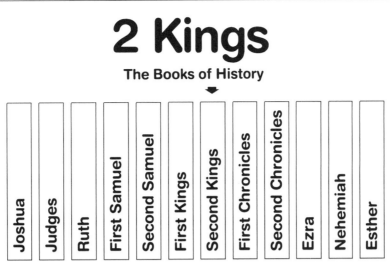

Joshua | Judges | Ruth | First Samuel | Second Samuel | First Kings | Second Kings | First Chronicles | Second Chronicles | Ezra | Nehemiah | Esther

Purpose/Theme:
Second Kings was written to record the last years of the Jewish people as a nation, and its captivity by the Babylonians in 586 B.C.

Key Verse:
"The Lord rejected all the people of Israel; he afflicted them and gave them into the hands of plunderers, until he thrust them from his presence" (17:20).

Main People:
In ISRAEL—Elijah, Jehu, Jeroboam II
In JUDAH—Joash, Ahaz, Hezekiah, Isaiah, Manasseh, Josiah

Outline:
☐ The ministry of Elijah (1 Kings 17—22; 2 Kings 1,2) ☐ The last days of Israel (2 Kings 10—17)
☐ The ministry of Elisha (2 Kings 1—9:13) ☐ The last days of Judah (2 Kings 18—25)

When Events Happened

(I)=KING OF ISRAEL (J)=KING OF JUDAH

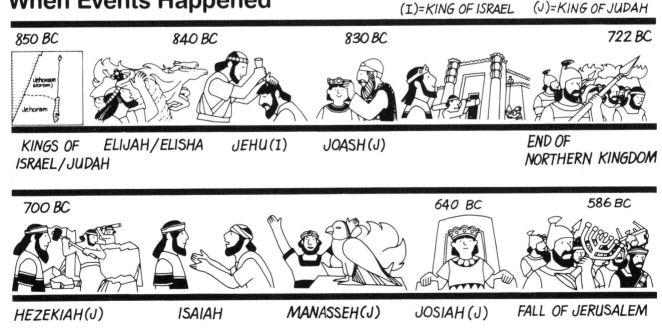

850 BC 840 BC 830 BC 722 BC

KINGS OF ISRAEL/JUDAH ELIJAH/ELISHA JEHU(I) JOASH(J) END OF NORTHERN KINGDOM

700 BC 640 BC 586 BC

HEZEKIAH(J) ISAIAH MANASSEH(J) JOSIAH(J) FALL OF JERUSALEM

Assyrian Compaigns against Israel and Judah

The Assyrian invasions of the eighth century B.C. were the most traumatic political events in the entire history of Israel.

The brutal Assyrian style of warfare relied on massive armies, superbly equipped with the world's first great siege machines manipulated by an efficient corps of engineers.

Psychological terror, however, was Assyria's most effective weapon. It was ruthlessly applied, with

corpses impaled on stakes, severed heads stacked in heaps, and captives skinned alive.

The shock of bloody military sieges on both Israel and Judah was profound. The prophets did not fail to scream out against their horror, while at the same time pleading with the people to see God's hand in history, to recognize spiritual causes in the present punishment.

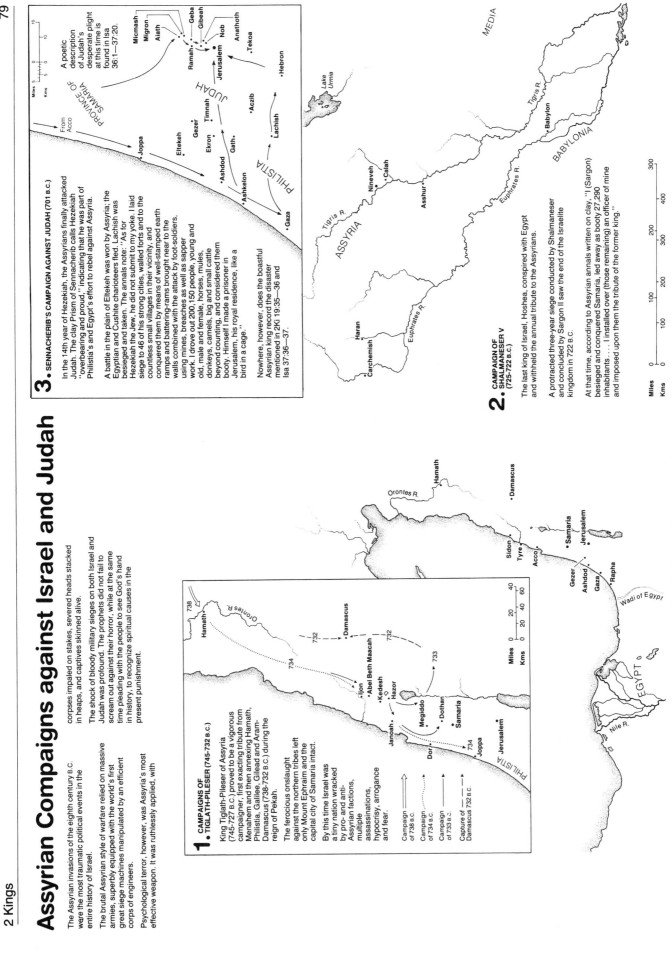

1. CAMPAIGNS OF TIGLATH-PILESER (745-732 B.C.)

King Tiglath-Pileser of Assyria (745-727 B.C.) proved to be a vigorous campaigner, first exacting tribute from Menahem and then annexing Hamath, Philistia, Galilee, Gilead and Aram-Damascus (738-732 B.C.) during the reign of Pekah.

The ferocious onslaught against the northern tribes left only Mount Ephraim and the capital city of Samaria intact.

By this time Israel was a tiny nation wracked by pro- and anti-Assyrian factions, multiple assassinations, hypocrisy, arrogance and fear.

Campaign of 738 B.C.
Campaign of 734 B.C.
Campaign of 733 B.C.
Capture of Damascus 732 B.C.

2. CAMPAIGN OF SHALMANESER V (725-722 B.C.)

The last king of Israel, Hoshea, conspired with Egypt and withheld the annual tribute to the Assyrians.

A protracted three-year siege conducted by Shalmaneser and concluded by Sargon II saw the end of the Israelite kingdom in 722 B.C.

At that time, according to Assyrian annals written on clay, "I (Sargon) besieged and conquered Samaria, led away as booty 27,290 inhabitants. . . . I installed over (those remaining) an officer of mine and imposed upon them the tribute of the former king."

3. SENNACHERIB'S CAMPAIGN AGAINST JUDAH (701 B.C.)

In the 14th year of Hezekiah, the Assyrians finally attacked Judah. The clay Prism of Sennacherib calls Hezekiah "overbearing and proud," indicating that he was part of Philistia's and Egypt's effort to rebel against Assyria.

A battle in the plain of Eltekeh was won by Assyria; the Egyptian and Cushite charioteers fled. Lachish was besieged and taken. The annals note: "As for Hezekiah the Jew, he did not submit to my yoke. I laid siege to 46 of his strong cities, walled forts and to the countless small villages in their vicinity, and conquered them by means of well-stamped earth ramps and battering-rams brought near to the walls combined with the attack by foot-soldiers, using mines, breaches as well as sapper work. I drove out 200,150 people, young and old, male and female, horses, mules, donkeys, camels, big and small cattle beyond counting, and considered them booty. Himself I made a prisoner in Jerusalem, his royal residence, like a bird in a cage."

Nowhere, however, does the boastful Assyrian king record the disaster mentioned in 2Ki 19:35—36 and Isa 37:36—37.

A poetic description of Judah's desperate plight at this time is found in Isa 36:1—37:20.

Exile of Northern Kingdom

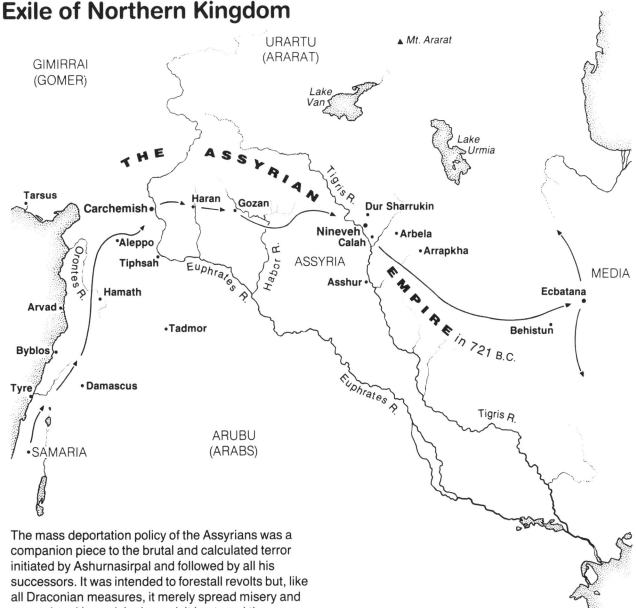

The mass deportation policy of the Assyrians was a companion piece to the brutal and calculated terror initiated by Ashurnasirpal and followed by all his successors. It was intended to forestall revolts but, like all Draconian measures, it merely spread misery and engendered hatred. In the end, it hastened the disintegration of the Assyrian empire.

There is some evidence that Israel experienced its first deportations under Tiglath-Pileser III (745-727 B.C.), a cruelty repeated by Sargon II (722-705 B.C.) at the time of the fall of Samaria. The latter king's inscriptions boast of carrying away 27,290 inhabitants of the city "as booty." According to 2Ki 17:6, they were sent to Assyria, to Halah (Calah?), to Gozan on the Habor River, and apparently to the eastern frontiers of the empire (to the towns of the Medes, most probably somewhere in the vicinity of Ecbatana, the modern Hamadan).

The sequel is provided by the inscriptions of Sargon: "The Arabs who live far away in the desert, who know neither overseers nor officials, and who had not yet brought their tribute to any king, I deported . . . and settled them in Samaria."

Much mythology has developed around the theme of the so-called ten lost tribes of Israel. A close examination of Assyrian records reveals that the deportations approximated only a limited percentage of the population, usually consisting of noble families. Agricultural workers, no doubt the majority, were deliberately left to care for the crops (cf. the Babylonian practice, 2Ki 24:14; 25:12).

Nebuchadnezzar's Campaign against Judah

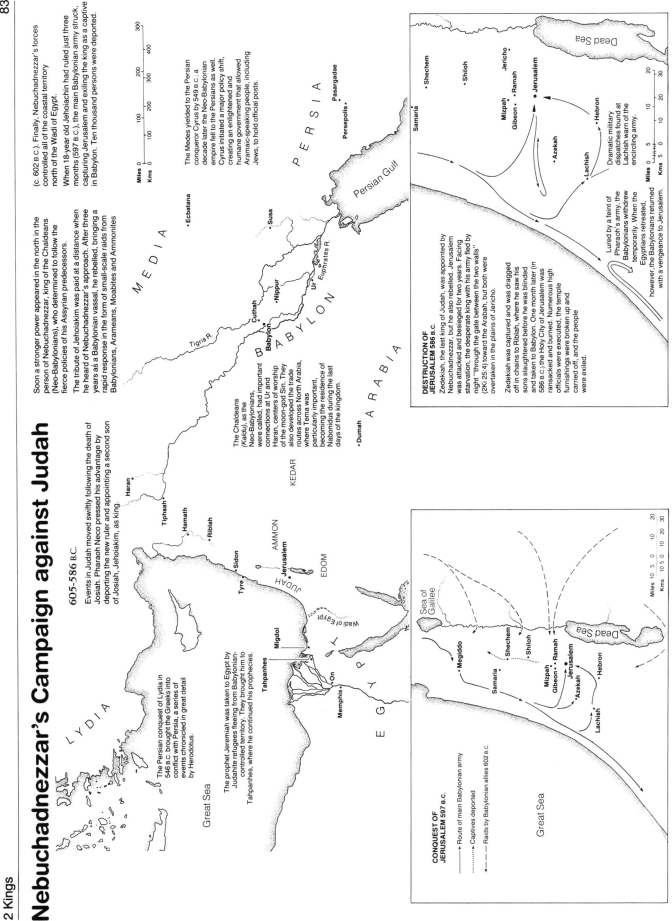

605–586 B.C.

Events in Judah moved swiftly following the death of Josiah. Pharaoh Neco pressed his advantage by deporting the new ruler and appointing a second son of Josiah, Jehoiakim, as king.

Soon a stronger power appeared in the north in the person of Nebuchadnezzar, king of the Chaldeans (Neo-Babylonians), who determined to follow the fierce policies of his Assyrian predecessors.

The tribute of Jehoiakim was paid at a distance when he heard of Nebuchadnezzar's approach. After three years as a Babylonian vassal, he rebelled, bringing a rapid response in the form of small-scale raids from Babylonians, Arameans, Moabites and Ammonites

(c. 602 B.C.). Finally, Nebuchadnezzar's forces controlled all of the coastal territory north of the Wadi of Egypt.

When 18-year old Jehoiachin had ruled just three months (597 B.C.), the main Babylonian army struck, capturing Jerusalem and exiling the king as a captive in Babylon. Ten thousand persons were deported.

The Medes yielded to the Persian conqueror Cyrus by 549 B.C.; a decade later the Neo-Babylonian empire fell to the Persians as well. Cyrus initiated a major policy shift, creating an enlightened and humane government that allowed Aramaic-speaking people, including Jews, to hold official posts.

The Persian conquest of Lydia in 546 B.C. brought the Greeks into conflict with Persia, a series of events chronicled in great detail by Herodotus.

The prophet Jeremiah was taken to Egypt by Judahite refugees fleeing from Babylonian-controlled territory. They brought him to Tahpanhes, where he continued his prophecies.

The Chaldeans (Kaldu), as the Neo-Babylonians, were called, had important connections at Ur and Haran, centers of worship of the moon-god Sin. They also developed the trade routes across North Arabia, where Tema was particularly important, becoming the residence of Nabonidus during the last days of the kingdom.

CONQUEST OF JERUSALEM 597 B.C.

Route of main Babylonian army

Captives deported

Raids by Babylonian allies 602 B.C.

DESTRUCTION OF JERUSALEM 586 B.C.

Zedekiah, the last king of Judah, was appointed by Nebuchadnezzar, but he also rebelled. Jerusalem was attacked and besieged for two years. Facing starvation, the desperate king with his army fled by night "through the gate between the two walls" (2Ki 25:4) toward the Arabah, but both were overtaken in the plains of Jericho.

Zedekiah was captured and was dragged off in chains to Riblah, where he was blinded and taken to Babylon. One month later (in 586 B.C.) the Holy City of Jerusalem was ransacked and burned. Numerous high officials were executed, the temple furnishings were broken up and carried off, and the people were exiled.

Lured by a feint of Pharaoh's army, the Babylonians withdrew temporarily. When the Egyptians retreated, however, the Babylonians returned with a vengeance to Jerusalem.

Dramatic military dispatches found at Lachish warn of the encircling army.

Exile of the Southern Kingdom

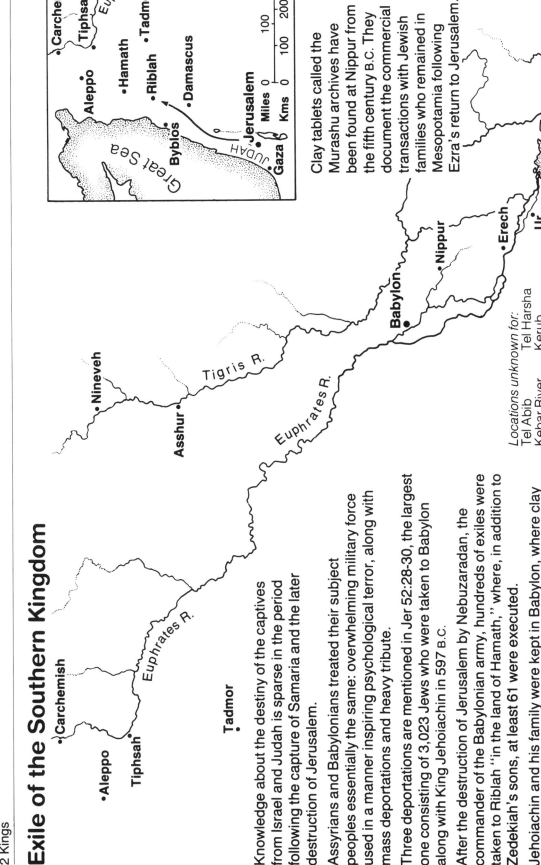

Knowledge about the destiny of the captives from Israel and Judah is sparse in the period following the capture of Samaria and the later destruction of Jerusalem.

Assyrians and Babylonians treated their subject peoples essentially the same: overwhelming military force used in a manner inspiring psychological terror, along with mass deportations and heavy tribute.

Three deportations are mentioned in Jer 52:28-30, the largest one consisting of 3,023 Jews who were taken to Babylon along with King Jehoiachin in 597 B.C.

After the destruction of Jerusalem by Nebuzaradan, the commander of the Babylonian army, hundreds of exiles were taken to Riblah "in the land of Hamath," where, in addition to Zedekiah's sons, at least 61 were executed.

Jehoiachin and his family were kept in Babylon, where clay ration receipts bearing his name have been found in a dramatic archaeological confirmation of Biblical history.

Eze 1:1-3 and 3:15 indicate that other captives were placed at Tel Abib and at the Kebar River, both probably in the locale of Nippur, as were other villages mentioned in Ezr 2:59; 8:15, 17; Ne 7:61.

Clay tablets called the Murashu archives have been found at Nippur from the fifth century B.C. They document the commercial transactions with Jewish families who remained in Mesopotamia following Ezra's return to Jerusalem.

Locations unknown for:

Tel Abib	Tel Harsha
Kebar River	Kerub
Ahava Canal	Addon
Casiphia	Immer
Tel Melah	

1 Chronicles

The Books of History

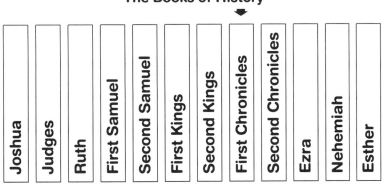

Joshua | Judges | Ruth | First Samuel | Second Samuel | First Kings | Second Kings | First Chronicles | Second Chronicles | Ezra | Nehemiah | Esther

Purpose/Theme:
The two books of Chronicles retell much of the history in 1 and 2 Kings, especially for those of the southern kingdom, Judah, who were allowed to return from Babylonian exile. First Chronicles dwells on the reign of King David.

Key Verse:
"David . . . said to Solomon his son, 'Be strong and courageous, and do the work. Do not be afraid or discouraged, for the Lord God, my God, is with you" (28:20).

Main People:
Adam, Abraham, Jacob, Saul, David

Outline:
☐ Lists of families and leaders (1 Chronicles 1—9)
☐ The reign of David (1 Chronicles 10—29)
- The death of Saul (1 Chronicles 10)
- David's rise to power (1 Chronicles 11,12)
- The ark of the covenant (1 Chronicles 13—16)
- God's promise and David's prayer (1 Chronicles 17)
- The victories of David (1 Chronicles 18—20)
- David's Census (1 Chronicles 21)
- Preparations for the Temple (1 Chronicles 22—27)
- David's last days and death (1 Chronicles 28,29)

When Events Happened

FIRST CHRONICLES

1010 BC

970 BC

Long live King Solomon!

SAUL   DAVID   NATHAN   SOLOMON

2 Chronicles

The Books of History ⬇

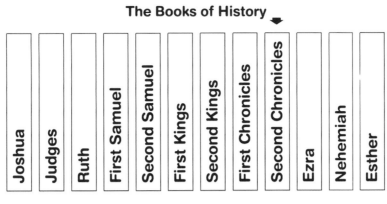

Joshua | Judges | Ruth | First Samuel | Second Samuel | First Kings | Second Kings | First Chronicles | Second Chronicles | Ezra | Nehemiah | Esther

Purpose/Theme:
To continue retelling of the history of Judah under King Solomon, with special focus on the Temple and the neglect of true worship.

Key Verse:
"But will God really dwell on earth with men? The heavens, even the highest heavens, cannot contain you. How much less this temple I have built!" (6:18)

Main People:
Solomon and the rulers of Judah

Outline:
☐ The numbers in parentheses are chapter numbers.
☐ The reign of Solomon (1—9)
  • Solomon's request (1)
  • Solomon's Temple (2—7)
  • Solomon's success (8,9)
☐ The rulers of Judah (10—36)
  • Rehoboam (10—12)
  • Abijah (13)
  • Asa (14—16)
  • Jehoshaphat (17—20)

• Jehoram (21)
• Ahaziah, Athaliah
• Joash (22—24)
• Amaziah (25)
• Uzziah (26)
• Jotham (27)
• Ahaz (28)
• Hezekiah (29—32)
• Manasseh, Amon (33)
• The fall of Jerusalem (36)

When Events Happened

SECOND CHRONICLES

| | 605 BC | 586 BC | 538 BC |

| DIVIDED KINGDOM | CAPTIVES TAKEN TO BABYLON | FALL OF JERUSALEM | CYRUS |

Ezra
The Books of History

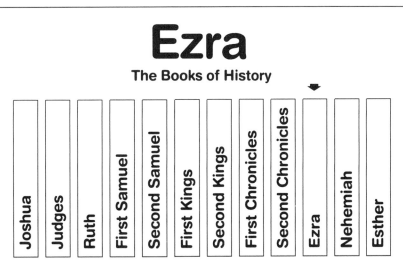

Joshua · Judges · Ruth · First Samuel · Second Samuel · First Kings · Second Kings · First Chronicles · Second Chronicles · Ezra · Nehemiah · Esther

Purpose/Theme:
The Babylonians are now conquered by the Persians. This account is of Ezra the priest being allowed to lead a return to Palestine in the fifth century B.C., to rebuild the Temple at Jerusalem.

Key Verse:
"The Lord our God has been gracious in leaving us a remnant and giving us a firm place in his sanctuary, and so our God gives light to our eyes and a little relief in our bondage" (9:8).

Main People:
Sheshbazzar, Ezra

Outline:
☐ The return under Sheshbazzar (Ezra 1—6)
- The decree of the Persian king (Ezra 1)
- The census of the people (Ezra 2)
- The rebuilding of the Temple (Ezra 3—6)

☐ The return under Ezra (Ezra 7—10)
- The return to Jerusalem (Ezra 7,8)
- Dealing with the people's sins (Ezra 9,10)

When Events Happened

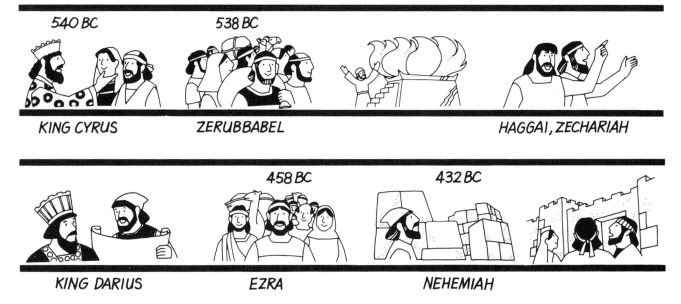

540 BC — KING CYRUS
538 BC — ZERUBBABEL
HAGGAI, ZECHARIAH

KING DARIUS
458 BC — EZRA
432 BC — NEHEMIAH

Chronology: Ezra-Nehemiah

Dates below are given according to a Nisan-to-Nisan Jewish calendar
(see chart on "Hebrew Calendar," p. 21).

Roman numerals represent months; Arabic numerals represent days.

540B.C.

530

YEAR	MONTH	DAY	EVENT	REFERENCE
539 B.C.	Oct.	12	Capture of Babylon	Da 5:30
538	Mar.	24	Cyrus's first year	Ezr 1:1-4
537	to Mar.	11		
537(?)			Return under Sheshbazzar	Ezr 1:11
537	VII		Building of altar	Ezr 3:1
536	II		Work on temple begun	Ezr 3:8
536-530			Opposition during Cyrus's reign	Ezr 4:1-5
530-520			Work on temple ceased	Ezr 4:24
520	VI =Sept.	24 21	Work on temple renewed under Darius	Ezr 5:2; Hag 1:14
516	XII =Mar.	3 12	Temple completed	Ezr 6:15

520

510

500

490

480

YEAR	MONTH	DAY	EVENT	REFERENCE
458	I =Apr.	1 8	Ezra departs from Babylon	Ezr 7:6-9
	V =Aug.	1 4	Ezra arrives in Jerusalem	Ezr 7:8-9
	IX =Dec.	20 19	People assemble	Ezr 10:9
	X =Dec.	1 29	Committee begins investigation	Ezr 10:16
457	I =Mar.	1 27	Committee ends investigation	Ezr 10:17
445 444	Apr. to Apr.	13 2	20th year of Artaxerxes I	Ne 1:1
445	I =Mar.-Apr.		Nehemiah approaches king	Ne 2:1
	Aug.(?)		Nehemiah arrives in Jerusalem	Ne 2:11
	VI =Oct.	25 2	Completion of wall	Ne 6:15
	VII =Oct. to Nov.	8 5	Public assembly	Ne 7:73-8:1
	VII =Oct.	15-22 22-28	Feast of Tabernacles	Ne 8:14
	VII =Oct.	24 30	Fast	Ne 9:1
433 432	Apr. to Apr.	1 19	32nd year of Artaxerxes; Nehemiah's recall and return	Ne 5:14; 13:6

470

460

450

440

430B.C.

Return from Exile

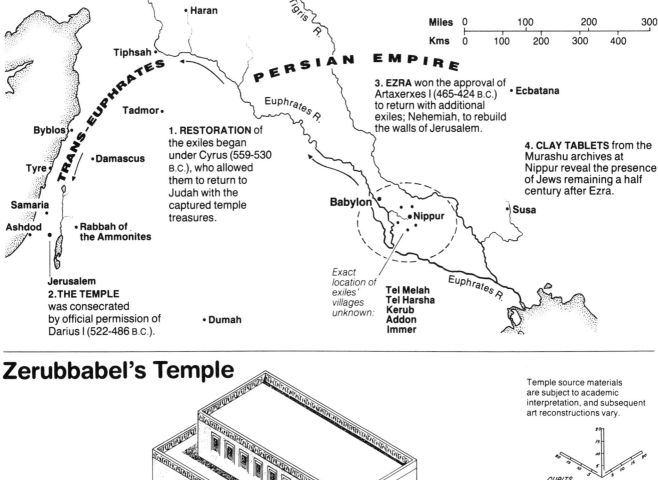

1. RESTORATION of the exiles began under Cyrus (559-530 B.C.), who allowed them to return to Judah with the captured temple treasures.

2. THE TEMPLE was consecrated by official permission of Darius I (522-486 B.C.).

3. EZRA won the approval of Artaxerxes I (465-424 B.C.) to return with additional exiles; Nehemiah, to rebuild the walls of Jerusalem.

4. CLAY TABLETS from the Murashu archives at Nippur reveal the presence of Jews remaining a half century after Ezra.

Exact location of exiles' villages unknown: **Tel Melah Tel Harsha Kerub Addon Immer**

Zerubbabel's Temple

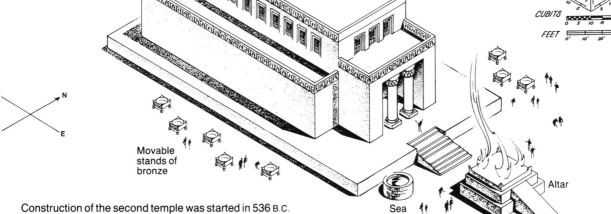

Temple source materials are subject to academic interpretation, and subsequent art reconstructions vary.

Movable stands of bronze

Sea

Altar

Construction of the second temple was started in 536 B.C. on the Solomonic foundations leveled a half-century earlier by the Babylonians. People who remembered the earlier temple wept at the comparison (Ezr 3:12). Not until 516 B.C., the 6th year of the Persian emperor Darius I (522-486), was the temple finally completed at the urging of Haggai and Zechariah (Ezr 6:13-15).

Archaeological evidence confirms that the Persian period in Palestine was a comparatively impoverished one in terms of material culture. Later Aramaic documents from Elephantine in Upper Egypt illustrate the official process of gaining permission to construct a Jewish place of worship, and the opposition engendered by the presence of various foes during this period.

Of the temple and its construction, little is known. Among the few contemporary buildings, the Persian palace at Lachish and the Tobiad monument at Iraq el-Amir may be compared in terms of technique.

Unlike the more famous structures razed in 586 B.C. and A.D. 70, the temple begun by Zerubbabel suffered no major hostile destruction, but was gradually repaired and reconstructed over a long period. Eventually it was replaced entirely by Herod's magnificent edifice.

Nehemiah

The Books of History

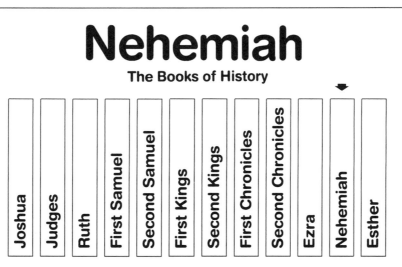

Joshua | Judges | Ruth | First Samuel | Second Samuel | First Kings | Second Kings | First Chronicles | Second Chronicles | Ezra | Nehemiah | Esther

Purpose/Theme:

Only a few years after Ezra served as a priest during the "restoration" of the Jews from Babylon, Nehemiah followed as governor. This book describes his leadership in rebuilding the walls of Jerusalem and renewing the covenant.

Key Verse:

"So we rebuilt the wall till all of it reached half its height, for the people worked with all their heart" (4:6).

Main Person:

Nehemiah

Outline:

☐ The rebuilding of the wall of Jerusalem (Nehemiah 1—7)
☐ The repairing of the agreement with God (Nehemiah 8—10)
☐ The reforming of the nation (Nehemiah 11—13)

When Events Happened

458 BC   432 BC

KING DARIUS   EZRA   NEHEMIAH

Jerusalem of the Returning Exiles

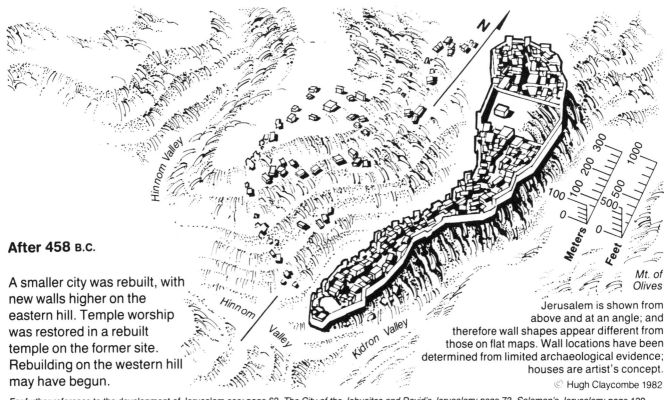

After 458 B.C.

A smaller city was rebuilt, with new walls higher on the eastern hill. Temple worship was restored in a rebuilt temple on the former site. Rebuilding on the western hill may have begun.

Jerusalem is shown from above and at an angle; and therefore wall shapes appear different from those on flat maps. Wall locations have been determined from limited archaeological evidence; houses are artist's concept.

© Hugh Claycombe 1982

For further reference to the development of Jerusalem see: page 63, *The City of the Jebusites and David's Jerusalem;* page 73, *Solomon's Jerusalem;* page 139, *Jerusalem During the Time of the Prophets.*

Nehemiah 2:11-20

I went to Jerusalem, and after staying there three days I set out during the night with a few men. I had not told anyone what my God had put in my heart to do for Jerusalem. There were no mounts with me except the one I was riding on.

By night I went out through the Valley Gate toward the Jackal Well and the Dung Gate, examining the walls of Jerusalem, which had been broken down, and its gates, which had been destroyed by fire. Then I moved on toward the Fountain Gate and the King's Pool, but there was not enough room for my mount to get through; so I went up the valley by night, examining the wall. Finally, I turned back and reentered through the Valley Gate. The officials did not know where I had gone or what I was doing, because as yet I had said nothing to the Jews or the priests or nobles or officials or any others who would be doing the work.

Then I said to them, "You see the trouble we are in: Jerusalem lies in ruins, and its gates have been burned with fire. Come, let us rebuild the wall of Jerusalem, and we will no longer be in disgrace." I also told them about the gracious hand of my God upon me and what the king had said to me.

They replied, "Let us start rebuilding." So they began this good work.

But when Sanballat the Horonite, Tobiah the Ammonite official and Geshem the Arab heard about it, they mocked and ridiculed us. "What is this you are doing?" they asked. "Are you rebelling against the king?"

I answered them by saying, "The God of heaven will give us success. We his servants will start rebuilding, but as for you, you have no share in Jerusalem or any claim or historic right to it."

Esther
The Books of History

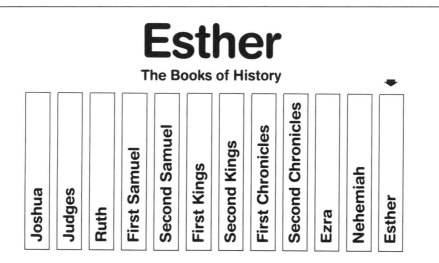

Joshua | Judges | Ruth | First Samuel | Second Samuel | First Kings | Second Kings | First Chronicles | Second Chronicles | Ezra | Nehemiah | Esther

Purpose/Theme:
To record God's preservation of the Jews through Esther, a Jewess who became queen of Persia, and the origins of the Feast of Purim in celebration of deliverance.

Key Verse:
"If you remain silent at this time, relief and deliverance for the Jews will arise from another place, but you and your father's family will perish. And who knows but that you have come to royal position for such a time as this?" (4:14).

Main People:
Vashti, Esther, Mordecai, Haman, Ahasuerus (Xerxes)

Outline:
☐ The rejection of Vashti (Esther 1)
☐ The crowning of Esther (Esther 2)
☐ The plotting of Haman (Esther 3,4)
☐ The courage of Esther (Esther 5)
☐ The deliverance of the Jews (Esther 6—10)

When Events Happened

460 BC

VASHTI   ESTHER   HAMAN / MORDECAI

Books of Poetry

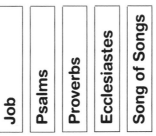

Job | Psalms | Proverbs | Ecclesiastes | Song of Songs

The five books of Hebrew poetry in our Old Testament contain some of the most inspiring writing in all literature. Their form reminds us that biblical faith is appropriately sung and celebrated, not just recited as historical fact.

Here the whole range of human emotions is exposed before God. There are complaints and weeping, questioning and rage, as well as praise and worship.

A special feature of this ancient poetry is that its "rhyming" is achieved by the repetition of thoughts, instead of sounds, as in English poetry. One line will state a truth in one way, and the next will build on that truth or restate it in a slightly different way. Psalm 19:1 is a good example:

"The heavens declare the glory of God;
The skies proclaim the work of his hands."

Some of this poetry is perhaps older than any other Old Testament writing. Some scholars, for example, believe the book of Job to have been written as far back as 2000 B.C. Many of the Psalms were written by David, a thousand years before Christ, and many of the Proverbs by Solomon, David's son. But since there are few historical references in the poetic books, no attempt is made to provide time lines here.

Job
The Books of Poetry

Purpose/Theme:
This is the most famous attempt in Western literature to grapple with the question of why good people some-times suffer. A part of the Old Covenant is that God will bless the faithful. Job agonizes over the apparent exceptions, trying to preserve both the power and the justice of God. The book concludes that ultimately the reason behind much suffering is known only to God.

Key Verse:
"As surely as God lives, who has denied me justice . . . as long as I have life within me, the breath of God in my nostrils, my lips will not speak wickedness, and my tongue will utter no deceit" (27:2-4).

Main People:
Job, his family, his friends (Eliphaz, Bildad, Zophar, Elihu).

Outline:
☐ The disasters of Job (Job 1,2)
☐ The friends of Job (Job 3—37)
☐ Job's conversation with God (Job 38—42)
☐ The deliverance of Job (Job 42)

When Events Happened

SOMEWHERE BETWEEN 2000~1000 BC

JOB   ELIPHAZ, BILDAD, ZOPHAR

ELIHU

Psalms

The Books of Poetry

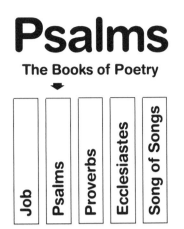

Purpose/Theme:
Most of the psalms were probably written to be set to music and sung. Because of their use in ancient Jewish worship, the book of Psalms is sometimes called the hymnbook of the Old Testament.

Key Verse:
"Shout for joy to the Lord, all the earth. Worship the Lord with gladness; come before him with joyful songs" (100:1-2).

Outline:
The book of Psalms is divided into five books, or collections of psalms.

Book	Psalms	Main Author or Collector
1	1-41	David
2	42-72	David/sons of Korah
3	73-89	Asaph
4	90-106	Unknown
5	107-150	David/Unknown

Asaph was David's choir leader. The sons of Korah were a family of official musicians.

Where to Find Psalms of:
Instruction: 1; 19; 39
Praise: 8; 29; 93; 100
Thanks: 30; 65; 103; 107; 116
Repentance: 6; 32; 38; 51; 130
Trust: 3; 27; 31; 46; 56; 62; 86
Distress: 4; 13; 55; 64; 88
Hope: 42; 63; 80; 84; 137
History: 78; 105; 106

Proverbs

The Books of Poetry

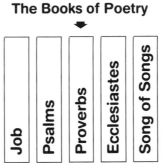

Purpose/Theme:

Proverbs is a part of the "wisdom" literature of the Old Testament. In its present form it is a collection of wise sayings from several sources, including King Solomon, laying practical rules for right living based on reverence for God instead of on mere human wisdom.

Key Verse:

"The fear of the Lord is the beginning of wisdom, and knowledge of the Holy One is understanding" (9:10).

Sample Topics:

The book of Proverbs has wise sayings for everyone to read and follow. These sayings deal with many different problems and situations. Most of the proverbs are very short and easy to remember. The proverbs are not organized in a way that puts all the sayings on one topic together. Instead, almost every verse raises a new and important idea.

- ☐ Respecting one's elders—Proverbs 1:8; 2:1; 3:1.
- ☐ The follow of unchaste love—Proverbs 2:16-19; chapter 5.
- ☐ The rewards of learning wisdom from God—Proverbs 2:1-15; 3:1-6.
- ☐ The value of discipline—Proverbs 6:23; 10:17; 15:5.
- ☐ The value of honesty—Proverbs 11:1,3; 20:10,23.
- ☐ The value of a good reputation—Proverbs 22:1.
- ☐ The fate of the fool—Proverbs 26:1,11,12
- ☐ The value of hard work—Proverbs 24:30-34; 26:13-16.

Ecclesiastes

The Books of Poetry

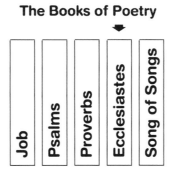

Purpose/Theme:

This pessimistic book, some of it from Solomon, is an experiment in the laboratory of life "under the sun"—that is, without reference to God. It concludes that without Him power, riches and wisdom are worth nothing—all is vanity.

Key Verse:

"Now all has been heard; here is the conclusion of the matter: fear God and keep his commandments, for this is the whole duty of man" (12:13).

Outline:

☐ The failure of the world to satisfy our longings (Ecclesiastes 1—4)
☐ The value of wisdom and reverence in the midst of vanity (Ecclesiastes 5—10)
☐ The conclusion of the matter (Ecclesiastes 11,12)

Song of Songs

The Books of Poetry

Job | Psalms | Proverbs | Ecclesiastes | Song of Songs

Purpose/Theme:
This romantic poetry celebrates human love in vivid, middle eastern imagery. It may have been written by Solomon about a favorite wife.

Key Verse:
"Love is as strong as death, its jealousy unyielding as the grave. It burns like blazing fire, like a mighty flame" (8:6).

Outline:
☐ Mutual expressions of love (Song of Songs 1—2)
☐ The pain of separation (Song of Songs 3)
☐ Images of love and beauty (Song of Songs 4—8)

Times of the Prophets

Books of Major Prophets

The Books of Minor Prophets

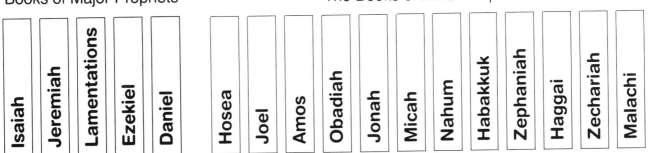

Isaiah | Jeremiah | Lamentations | Ezekiel | Daniel

Hosea | Joel | Amos | Obadiah | Jonah | Micah | Nahum | Habakkuk | Zephaniah | Haggai | Zechariah | Malachi

Israel's prophets are a built-in "reformation" aspect of Old Testament faith. The word "prophet" means "to speak out"—to *forth-tell* God's word as much as to foretell the future. They spoke out against hypocrisy, injustice, immorality and idolatry, warning God's people that He would punish them for such continued disobedience. The prophets also foretold the time when God would save a remnant of His people through whom all nations would be blessed.

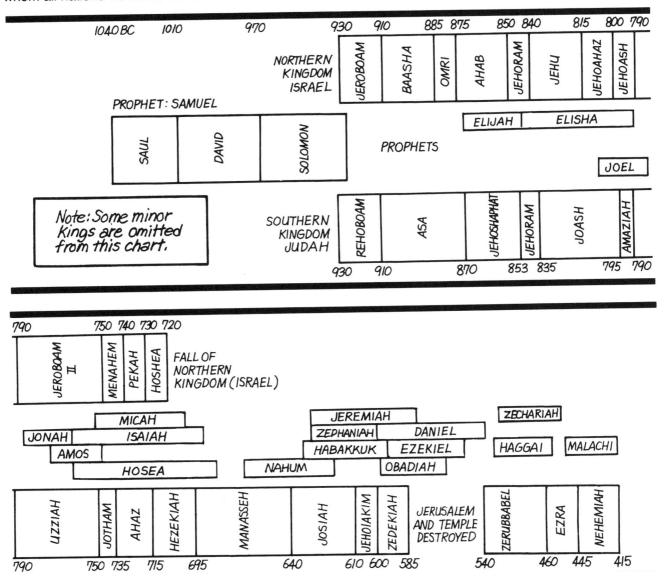

The Major Prophets

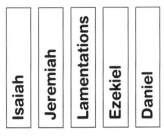

The term "major" prophets simply indicates that these five books are the longest books of prophecy in the Old Testament. If, as many scholars believe, Jeremiah was the author of Lamentations, there are actually only four "major *prophets*," and five "major *prophecies.*"

When Events Happened

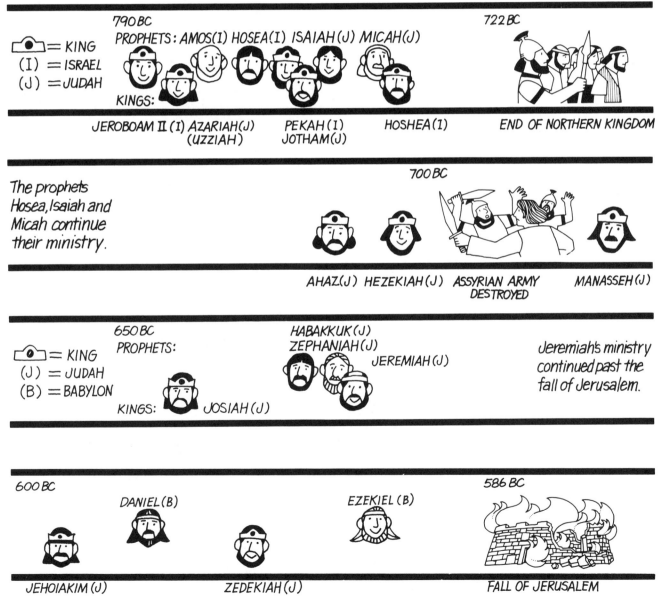

Isaiah

The Books of Major Prophets

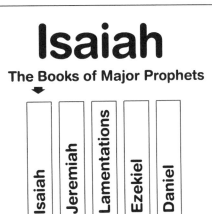

| Isaiah | Jeremiah | Lamentations | Ezekiel | Daniel |

Purpose/Theme:

Isaiah was a prophet in Judah during the eighth century, when the northern kingdom of Israel was conquered by the Assyrians. He is often called "the Messianic prophet," since his message of future judgment and deliverance pointed forward to the coming of Christ.

Key Verse:

"For to us a child is born, to us a son is given, and the government will be on his shoulders. And he will be called Wonderful Counselor, Mighty God, Everlasting Father, Prince of Peace" (9:6).

Main People:

Isaiah; the Judaean kings Uzziah, Jotham, Ahaz, Hezekiah and Manasseh.

Outline:

☐ God's messages of judgment (Isaiah 1-39)
  • Under Kings Uzziah and Jotham (Isaiah 1—6)
  • Under King Ahaz (Isaiah 7—14)
  • Under King Hezekiah (Isaiah 15—39)
☐ God's messages of comfort (Isaiah 40—66)
  • God's promise to free His people and bring them again to the land He gave them (Isaiah 40—52)
  • The coming of God's Servant (Jesus Christ) to be the Messiah King (Isaiah 52,53)
  • The future glory of God's people (Isaiah 54—66)

When Events Happened

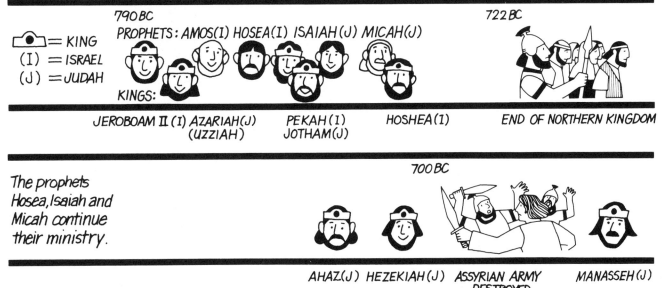

Jeremiah
The Books of Major Prophets

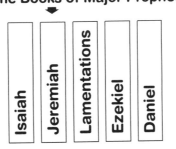

Purpose/Theme:
This records the prophet Jeremiah's tragically unsuccessful calls for Judah to repent of idolatry and immorality, thus avoiding Babylonian captivity; and his predictions that a remnant will be saved.

Key Verse:
"If you do not listen, I will weep in secret because of your pride; my eyes will weep bitterly, overflowing with tears, because the Lord's flock will be taken captive" (13:17).

Main People:
Jeremiah; important Judaean kings: Manasseh, Josiah, Zedekiah.

Outline:
☐ Before the fall of Jerusalem (Jeremiah 1—38)
☐ After the fall of Jerusalem (Jeremiah 39—52)

NOTE: The book of Jeremiah does not follow the order in which things happened. Jeremiah and his assistant, Baruch, wrote Jeremiah's messages on a long scroll. Probably, while writing down one message, Jeremiah would be reminded of another message he had spoken before. The earlier message would then be added to the scroll where he had left off writing. This mixing of early and late messages makes it very difficult to know the order in which his messages were given.

When Events Happened

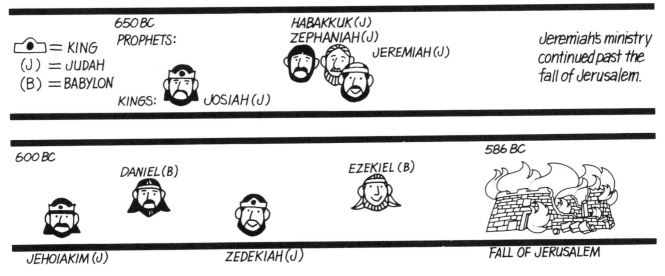

Lamentations

The Books of Major Prophets

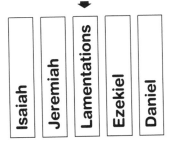

Purpose/Theme:

Lamentations is "a funeral dirge over the desolation of Jerusalem" (Halley), in 586 B.C., probably written by the prophet Jeremiah.

Key Verse:

"How deserted lies the city, once so full of people! How like a widow is she, who once was great among the nations! She who was queen among the provinces has now become a slave" (1:1).

Outline:

- ☐ The tragic state of Jerusalem (Lamentations 1)
- ☐ The wrath of God (Lamentations 2)
- ☐ Jeremiah's grief (Lamentations 3)
- ☐ The reason for the tragedy (Lamentations 4, 5)

When Events Happened

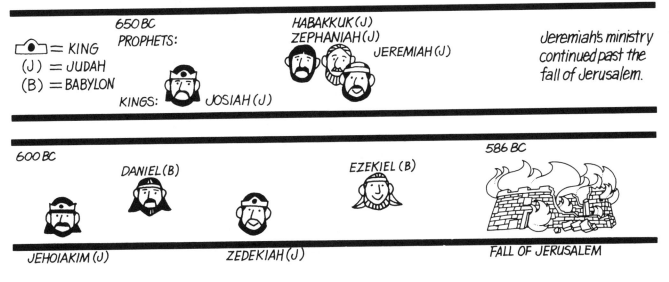

Ezekiel

The Books of Major Prophets

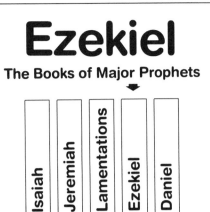

Purpose/Theme:

Ezekiel was a prophet of the Babylonian captivity. He was given visions and dreams about the fall of Jerusalem, God's wrath toward the nations and the return of a remnant from Babylon.

Key Verses:

"O my people, I am going to open your graves and bring you up from them; I will bring you back to the land of Israel . . . I will put my Spirit in you and you will live" (37:12,14).

Outline:

☐ Ezekiel's call (Ezekiel 1—3)
☐ Ezekiel's prophecies
  • against Judah and Jerusalem (Ezekiel 4—24)
  • against the nations (Ezekiel 25—32)
  • about Israel and the last days (Ezekiel 33—48)

When Events Happened

Dates in Ezekiel

REFERENCE	YEAR	MONTH	DAY	MODERN RECKONING	EVENT
1. 1:1 1:2 3:16	30 5 "At the end of seven days"	4 —	5 5	July 31, 593 B.C.	Inaugural vision
2. 8:1	6	6	5	Sept. 17, 592	Transport to Jerusalem
3. 20:1-2	7	5	10	Aug. 14, 591	Negative view of Israel's history
4. 24:1	9	10	10	Jan. 15, 588	Beginning of siege (see also 2 Ki 25:1)
5. 26:1	11	—	1	Apr. 23, 587 to Apr. 13, 586	Oracle against Tyre
6. 29:1	10	10	12	Jan. 7, 587	Oracle against Egypt
7. 29:17	27	1	1	Apr. 26, 571	Egypt in exchange for Tyre
8. 30:20	11	1	7	Apr. 29, 587	Oracle against Pharaoh
9. 31:1	11	3	1	June 21, 587	Oracle against Pharaoh
10. 32:1	12	12	1	Mar. 3, 585	Lament over Pharaoh
11. 32:17	12	—	15	Apr. 13, 586, to Apr. 1, 585	Egypt dead
12. 33:21	12	10	5	Jan. 8, 585	Arrival of first fugitive
13. 40:1 40:1	25 "fourteenth year after the fall of the city"	1	10	Apr. 28, 573	Vision of the future

Ezekiel's Temple

A. Wall (40:5,16-20)
B. East gate (40:6-14,16)
C. Portico (40:8)
D. Outer court (40:17)
E. Pavement (40:17)
F. Inner court (40:19)
G. North gate (40:20-22)

H. Inner court (40:23)
I. South gate (40:24-26)
J. South inner court (40:27)
K. Gateway (40:32-34)
L. Gateway (40:32-34)
M. Gateway (40:35-38)
N. Priests' rooms (40:44-45)

O. Court (40:47)
P. Temple portico (40:48-49)
Q. Outer sanctuary (41:1-2)
R. Most Holy Place (41:3-4)
S. Temple walls (41:5-7, 9, 11)
T. Base (41:8)
U. Open area (41:10)
V. West building (41:12)
W. Priests' rooms (42:1-10)
X. Altar (43:13-17)

AA. Rooms for preparing sacrifices (40:39-43)
BB. Ovens (46:19-20)
CC. Kitchens (46:21-24)

Ezekiel uses a long or "royal" cubit, 20.4 inches or 51.81 cm ("cubit and a handbreadth," Eze 40:5) as opposed to the standard Hebrew cubit of 17.6 inches or 44.7 cm.

Scripture describes a floor plan, but provides few height dimensions. This artwork shows an upward projection of the temple over the floor plan. This temple existed only in a vision of Ezekiel (Eze 40:2), and has never actually been built as were the temples of Solomon, Zerubbabel and Herod.

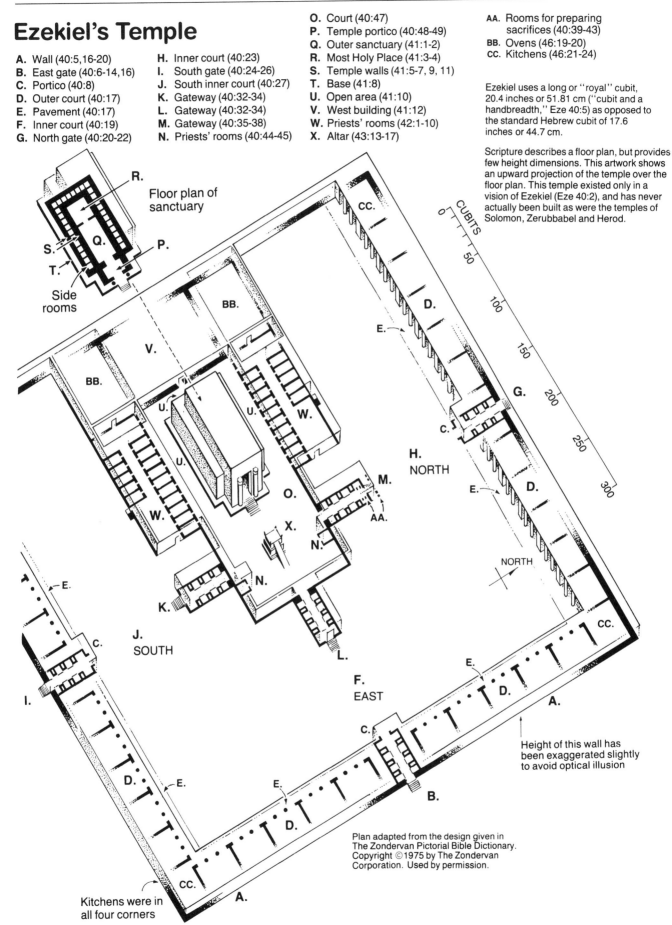

Floor plan of sanctuary

Side rooms

Height of this wall has been exaggerated slightly to avoid optical illusion

Plan adapted from the design given in The Zondervan Pictorial Bible Dictionary. Copyright ©1975 by The Zondervan Corporation. Used by permission.

Kitchens were in all four corners

Daniel
The Books of Major Prophets

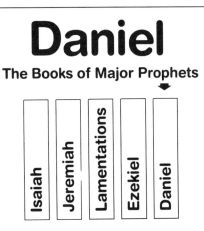

Purpose/Theme:
This book is the story of some Hebrew captives who gained the favor of both God and their captors. Daniel's visions and dreams symbolize the sovereignty of God and His coming kingdom over all the kingdoms of the earth.

Key Verse:
"In the time of those kings, the God of heaven will set up a kingdom that will never be destroyed, nor will it be left to another people. It will crush all those kingdoms and bring them to an end, but it will itself endure forever" (2:44).

Main People:
Daniel, Shadrach, Meshach, Abednego; King Nebuchadnezzar.

Outline:
☐ Daniel's life in Babylon (Daniel 1—6)
- Daniel, a young man in Babylon (Daniel 1)
- Nebuchadnezzar's dream: the great image (Daniel 2)
- The fiery furnace (Daniel 3)
- Nebuchadnezzar's dream: a great tree (Daniel 4)
- Belshazzar: the handwriting on the wall (Daniel 5)
- Daniel in the lion's den (Daniel 6)

☐ Daniel's visions (Daniel 7—12)

When Events Happened

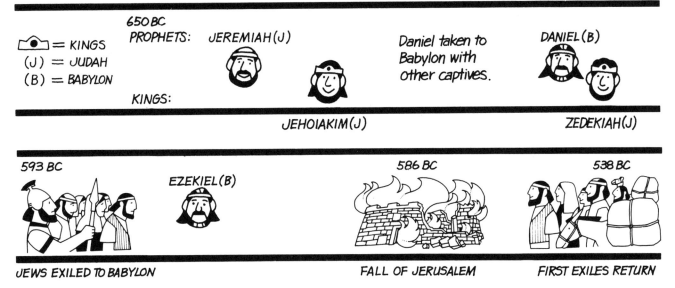

Identification of the Four Kingdoms
Chronology of Major Empires in Daniel

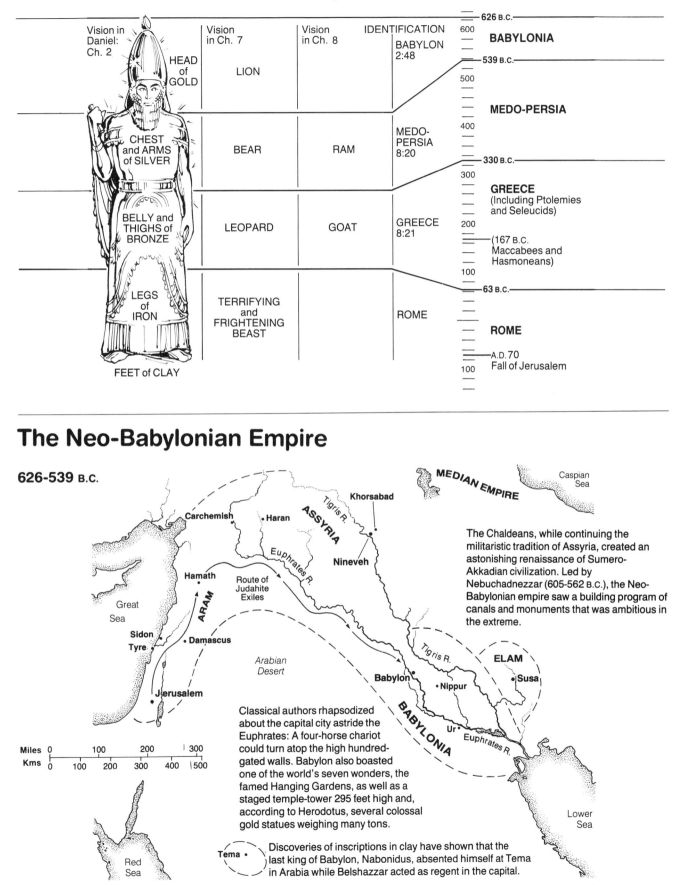

Vision in Daniel: Ch. 2	Vision in Ch. 7	Vision in Ch. 8	IDENTIFICATION	
HEAD of GOLD	LION		BABYLON 2:48	626 B.C. **BABYLONIA**
CHEST and ARMS of SILVER	BEAR	RAM	MEDO-PERSIA 8:20	539 B.C. **MEDO-PERSIA**
BELLY and THIGHS of BRONZE	LEOPARD	GOAT	GREECE 8:21	330 B.C. **GREECE** (Including Ptolemies and Seleucids) (167 B.C. Maccabees and Hasmoneans)
LEGS of IRON / FEET of CLAY	TERRIFYING and FRIGHTENING BEAST		ROME	63 B.C. **ROME** A.D. 70 Fall of Jerusalem

The Neo-Babylonian Empire

626-539 B.C.

The Chaldeans, while continuing the militaristic tradition of Assyria, created an astonishing renaissance of Sumero-Akkadian civilization. Led by Nebuchadnezzar (605-562 B.C.), the Neo-Babylonian empire saw a building program of canals and monuments that was ambitious in the extreme.

Classical authors rhapsodized about the capital city astride the Euphrates: A four-horse chariot could turn atop the high hundred-gated walls. Babylon also boasted one of the world's seven wonders, the famed Hanging Gardens, as well as a staged temple-tower 295 feet high and, according to Herodotus, several colossal gold statues weighing many tons.

Discoveries of inscriptions in clay have shown that the last king of Babylon, Nabonidus, absented himself at Tema in Arabia while Belshazzar acted as regent in the capital.

Miles 0   100   200   300
Kms 0   100   200   300   400   500

Ptolemies and Seleucids

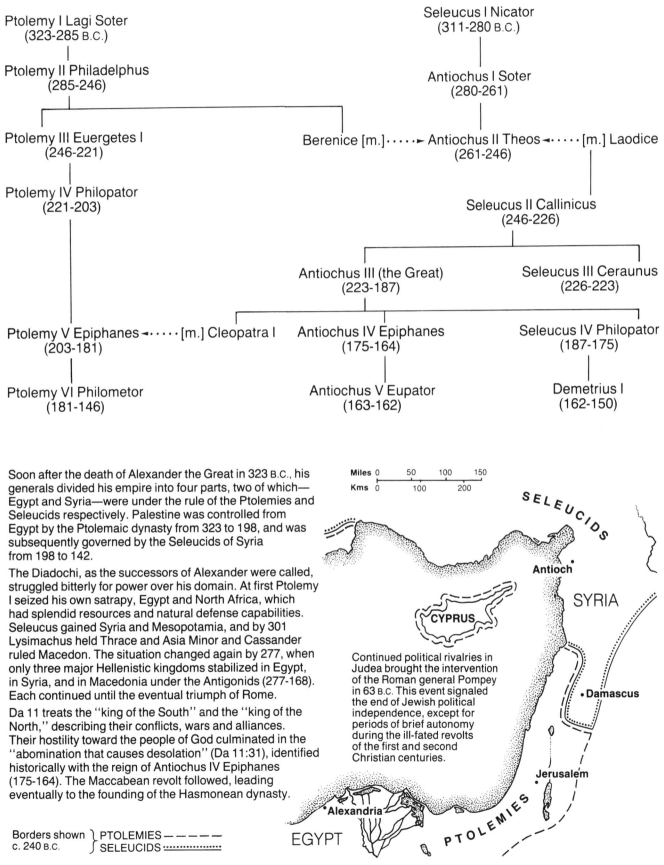

Ptolemy I Lagi Soter
(323-285 B.C.)

Seleucus I Nicator
(311-280 B.C.)

Ptolemy II Philadelphus
(285-246)

Antiochus I Soter
(280-261)

Ptolemy III Euergetes I
(246-221)

Berenice [m.]·····► Antiochus II Theos ◄····· [m.] Laodice
(261-246)

Ptolemy IV Philopator
(221-203)

Seleucus II Callinicus
(246-226)

Antiochus III (the Great)
(223-187)

Seleucus III Ceraunus
(226-223)

Ptolemy V Epiphanes ◄····· [m.] Cleopatra I
(203-181)

Antiochus IV Epiphanes
(175-164)

Seleucus IV Philopator
(187-175)

Ptolemy VI Philometor
(181-146)

Antiochus V Eupator
(163-162)

Demetrius I
(162-150)

Soon after the death of Alexander the Great in 323 B.C., his generals divided his empire into four parts, two of which—Egypt and Syria—were under the rule of the Ptolemies and Seleucids respectively. Palestine was controlled from Egypt by the Ptolemaic dynasty from 323 to 198, and was subsequently governed by the Seleucids of Syria from 198 to 142.

The Diadochi, as the successors of Alexander were called, struggled bitterly for power over his domain. At first Ptolemy I seized his own satrapy, Egypt and North Africa, which had splendid resources and natural defense capabilities. Seleucus gained Syria and Mesopotamia, and by 301 Lysimachus held Thrace and Asia Minor and Cassander ruled Macedon. The situation changed again by 277, when only three major Hellenistic kingdoms stabilized in Egypt, in Syria, and in Macedonia under the Antigonids (277-168). Each continued until the eventual triumph of Rome.

Da 11 treats the "king of the South" and the "king of the North," describing their conflicts, wars and alliances. Their hostility toward the people of God culminated in the "abomination that causes desolation" (Da 11:31), identified historically with the reign of Antiochus IV Epiphanes (175-164). The Maccabean revolt followed, leading eventually to the founding of the Hasmonean dynasty.

Miles 0   50   100   150
Kms 0   100   200

Continued political rivalries in Judea brought the intervention of the Roman general Pompey in 63 B.C. This event signaled the end of Jewish political independence, except for periods of brief autonomy during the ill-fated revolts of the first and second Christian centuries.

Borders shown ⎱ PTOLEMIES — — — —
c. 240 B.C. ⎰ SELEUCIS ·············

The Minor Prophets

Hosea | Joel | Amos | Obadiah | Jonah | Micah | Nahum | Habakkuk | Zephaniah | Haggai | Zechariah | Malachi

These twelve books of Old Testament prophecies are called the "minor" prophets because they are shorter than the "major" prophets (prophecies)—not because they are less important. Remember that the term "prophet" means to "forth-tell" God's word as much as to fore-tell the future.

When Events Happened

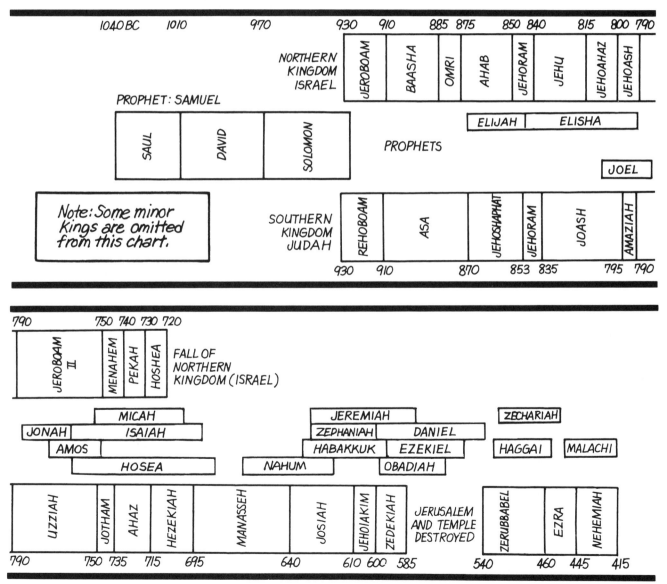

Jerusalem During the Time of the Prophets

c. 750-586 B.C.

Refugees arrived in Jerusalem about the time of the fall of the northern kingdom (722 B.C.). Settlement spread to the western hill, and a new wall was added for protection. Hezekiah carved an underground aqueduct out of solid rock to bring an ample water supply inside the city walls, enabling Jerusalem to survive the siege of Sennacherib in 701.

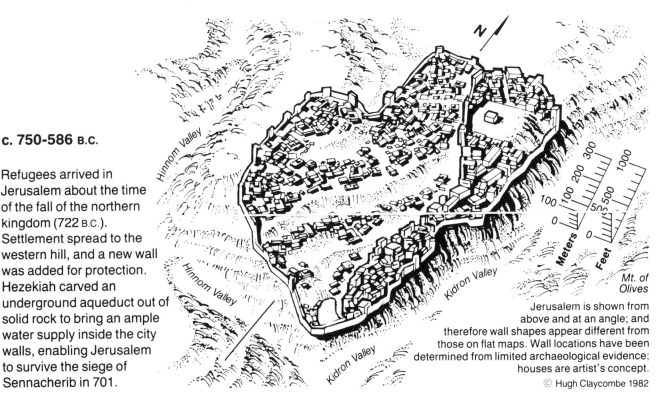

Jerusalem is shown from above and at an angle; and therefore wall shapes appear different from those on flat maps. Wall locations have been determined from limited archaeological evidence; houses are artist's concept.

© Hugh Claycombe 1982

"Oh Jerusalem, Jerusalem, you who kill the prophets and stone those sent to you, how often I have longed to gather your children together, as a hen gathers her chicks under her wings, but you were not willing. Look, your house is left to you desolate. For I tell you, you will not see me again until you say, 'Blessed is he who comes in the name of the Lord.'"—Matthew 23:37-39

For further reference to the development of Jerusalem see: page 63, *The City of the Jebusites and David's Jerusalem;* page 73, *Solomon's Jerusalem;* page 99, *Jerusalem of the Returning Exiles*

Hosea

The Books of Minor Prophets

Hosea | Joel | Amos | Obadiah | Jonah | Micah | Nahum | Habakkuk | Zephaniah | Haggai | Zechariah | Malachi

Purpose/Theme:

The prophet Hosea called the northern nation of Israel to repentance in the eighth century B.C. He emphasizes God's faithfulness or "covenant-love." But the people would not listen, and they were carried away into Assyrian captivity about the middle of Hosea's ministry.

Key Verse:

"The Lord said to [Hosea], 'Go, take to yourself an adulterous wife and children of unfaithfulness, because the land is guilty of the vilest adultery in departing from the Lord'" (1:2).

Main People:

Hosea; the kings of Israel from Jeroboam II to Hoshea.

Outline:

☐ Hosea's wife (Hosea 1—3)
☐ Hosea's people (Hosea 4—14)
  • The message of judgment (Hosea 4—10)
  • The message of love (Hosea 11—14)

When Events Happened

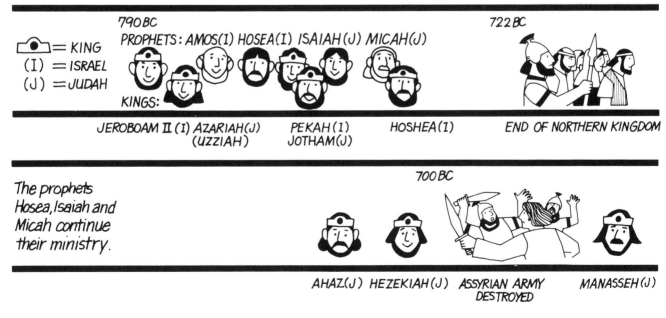

= KING
(I) = ISRAEL
(J) = JUDAH

790 BC
PROPHETS: AMOS(I) HOSEA(I) ISAIAH(J) MICAH(J)
KINGS:
722 BC

JEROBOAM II (I) AZARIAH(J)   PEKAH(I)   HOSHEA(I)   END OF NORTHERN KINGDOM
(UZZIAH)   JOTHAM(J)

The prophets
Hosea, Isaiah and
Micah continue
their ministry.

700 BC

AHAZ(J) HEZEKIAH(J) ASSYRIAN ARMY   MANASSEH(J)
DESTROYED

Joel
The Books of Minor Prophets

| Hosea | Joel | Amos | Obadiah | Jonah | Micah | Nahum | Habakkuk | Zephaniah | Haggai | Zechariah | Malachi |

Purpose/Theme:
A little before Hosea prophesied to Israel in the north, Joel preached to Judah in the south. He warned that a plague of locusts and a resulting famine stood for the judgment of the Day of the Lord that was to come, but that the Day would also come with an outpouring of God's Spirit.

Key Verses:
"I will pour out my Spirit on all people. Your sons and daughters will prophesy, your old men will dream dreams, your young men will see visions . . . And everyone who calls on the name of the Lord will be saved" (2:28,32).

Main People:
Joel; possibly during the reigns of King Joash or King Uzziah.

Outline:
☐ Looking back at God's judgment (Joel 1)
☐ Looking toward the Day of the Lord (Joel 2,3)

When Events Happened

```
                                        850 BC                                                    800 BC
    🔲 = KING          PROPHETS:                                              JOEL
   (I) = ISRAEL
   (J) = JUDAH
                       KINGS:
                                                     JEHU (I)    JOASH
```

Amos
The Books of Minor Prophets

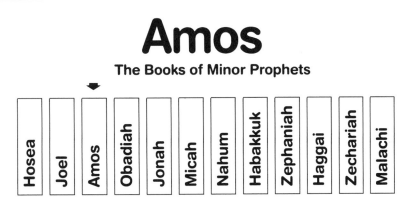

Purpose/Theme:
Amos was another eighth-century prophet with a message for the northern kingdom, Israel, although he lived in Judah. His visions and prophecies warned both the Jews and their persecutors of God's coming judgment, but also predicted the glory of a restored kingdom of David.

Key Verses:
"I hate, I despise your religious feasts; I cannot stand your assemblies . . . let justice roll on like a river, righteousness like a never-failing stream!" (5:21,24).

Main People:
Amos was a contemporary of Hosea, and, late in his ministry, of Isaiah and Micah. King Uzziah ruled in Judah and Jeroboam II in Israel.

Outline:
Amos's prophecies: warning the nations (Amos 1,2)
☐ Amos's sermons: speaking about Israel (Amos 3—6)
☐ Amos's visions: the future of Israel (Amos 7—9)

When Events Happened

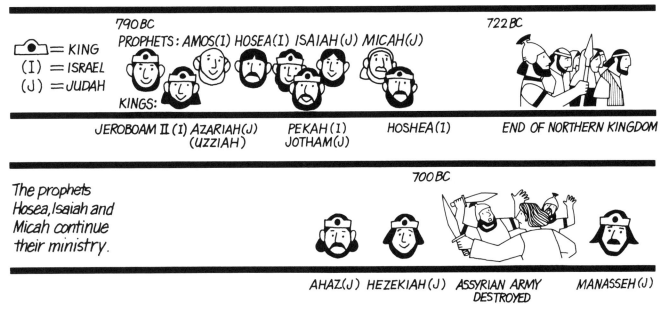

Obadiah
The Books of Minor Prophets

Hosea | Joel | Amos | Obadiah | Jonah | Micah | Nahum | Habakkuk | Zephaniah | Haggai | Zechariah | Malachi

Purpose/Theme:

This prophecy was directed toward the Edomites, descendants of Esau and long-time enemies of the Israelites. Edom was known for its rocky cliffs, which made natural fortresses. The Edomites were overrun by the Babylonians when they destroyed Jerusalem in the sixth century B.C., just as Obadiah predicted.

Key Verse:

"The pride of your heart has deceived you, you who live in the clefts of the rocks and make your home on the heights, you who say to yourself, 'Who can bring me down to the ground?'" (1:3).

Outline:

☐ Introduction (v. 1)
☐ Judgement on Edom (vv. 2-14)
☐ The Day of the Lord (vv. 15-21)

When Events Happened

600 BC   605 BC   593 BC   586 BC
PROPHETS: JEREMIAH (J)   DANIEL (B)   EZEKIEL (B) OBADIAH

KINGS:

JEHOIAKIM (J)   Daniel and others   ZEDEKIAH (J)   Ezekiel and others   FALL OF JERUSALEM
                       taken captive.   taken captive.

Jonah
The Books of Minor Prophets

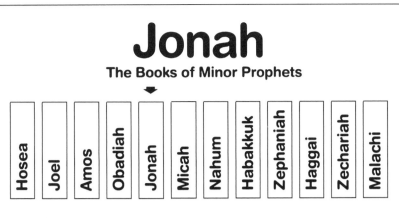

Purpose/Theme:
Jonah was another eighth-century prophet whom God sent to preach to the people of Nineveh—a city of the Assyrians, the very nation God had selected to punish the northern kingdom of Israel. No wonder Jonah fled, leading to the famous story of Jonah and the great fish.

Key Verse:
"Nineveh has more than a hundred and twenty thousand people who cannot tell their right hand from their left, and many cattle as well. Should I not be concerned about that great city?" (4:11).

Outline:
☐ Jonah tried to run away (Jonah 1)
☐ Jonah prayed to God (Jonah 2)
☐ Jonah preached to the people in Nineveh (Jonah 3)
☐ Jonah learned God loves all people (Jonah 4)

When Events Happened

The Book of Jonah

Nineveh and Tarshish represented opposite ends of the Levantine commercial sphere in ancient times. The story of Jonah extends to the boundaries of OT geographic knowledge and provides a rare glimpse of seafaring life in the Iron Age. Inscriptions and pottery from Spain demonstrate that Phoenician trade linked the far distant ends of the Mediterranean, perhaps as early as the 12th century B.C.

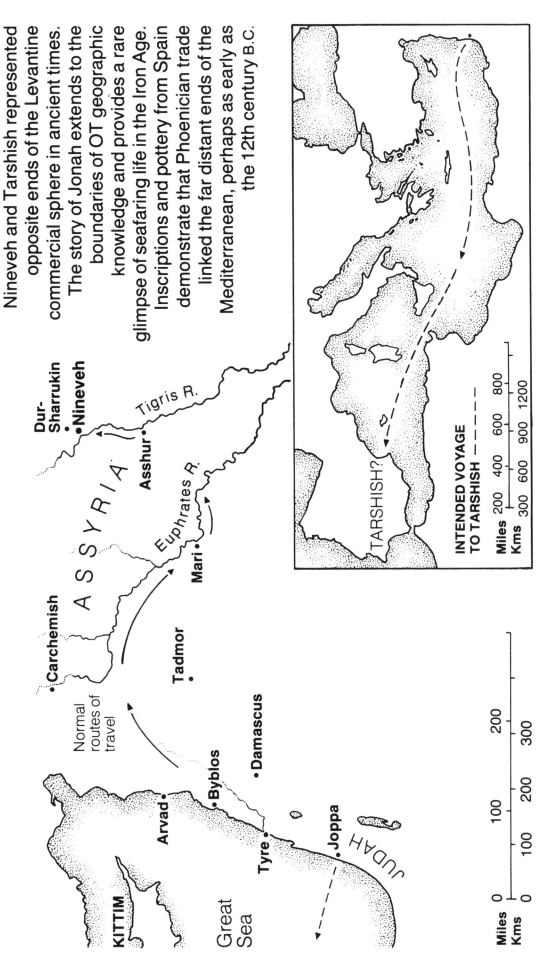

Micah

The Books of Minor Prophets

Hosea | Joel | Amos | Obadiah | Jonah | Micah | Nahum | Habakkuk | Zephaniah | Haggai | Zechariah | Malachi

Purpose/Theme:

About the time Isaiah was preaching to Jerusalem, Micah was prophesying in western Judah, directing his warnings to Israel as well.

Key Verse:

"In the last days the mountain of the Lord's temple will be established as chief among the mountains; it will be raised above the hills, and peoples will stream to it" (4:1).

Outline:

☐ Micah warned that nations and rulers who do not obey God will be defeated (Micah 1—3)
☐ Micah promised that God will provide a new King (Micah 4,5)
☐ Micah gave the people God's promise that He will forgive them (Micah 6,7)

When Events Happened

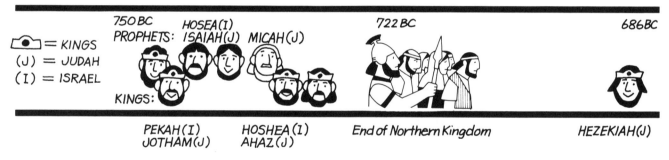

750 BC PROPHETS: HOSEA(I) ISAIAH(J) MICAH(J)   722 BC   686 BC

= KINGS
(J) = JUDAH
(I) = ISRAEL

KINGS:

PEKAH(I)   HOSHEA(I)   End of Northern Kingdom   HEZEKIAH(J)
JOTHAM(J)   AHAZ(J)

Nahum

The Books of Minor Prophets

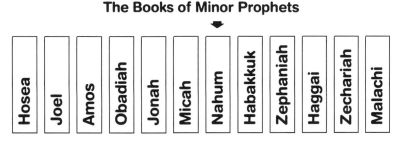

Hosea | Joel | Amos | Obadiah | Jonah | Micah | Nahum | Habakkuk | Zephaniah | Haggai | Zechariah | Malachi

Purpose/Theme:

Nahum preached of God's justice and love. Like Jonah, he warned that Nineveh would be destroyed because of its wickedness. Later, God would restore His people to the land of promise.

Key Promise:

"The Lord is good, a refuge in times of trouble. He cares for those who trust in him, but with an overwhelming flood he will make an end of Nineveh; he will pursue his foes into darkness" (1:7,8).

Outline:

☐ Nineveh's Judge (Nahum 1)
☐ Judgment (Nahum 2)
☐ Instruction (Nahum 3)

When Events Happened

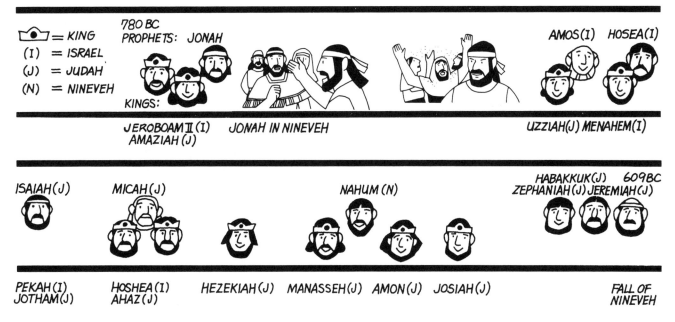

Habakkuk

The Books of Minor Prophets

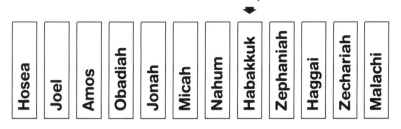

Purpose/Theme:

This book was written to show the justice of God in allowing such terrible judgment to come upon Judah by the hands of an equally wicked nation, Babylon. God assures Habakkuk that the Babylonians will also be punished, and that He will save those who are faithful to Him.

Key Verse:

"Lord, I have heard of your fame; I stand in awe of your deeds, O Lord. Renew them in our day, in our time make them known; in wrath remember mercy" (3:2).

Outline:

☐ The first complaint (Habakkuk 1:1-4)
☐ God's answer (Habakkuk 1:5-11)
☐ The second complaint (Habakkuk 1:12—2:1)
☐ God's answer (Habakkuk 2:2-20)
☐ A prayer of praise (Habakkuk 3)

When Events Happened

Zephaniah
The Books of Minor Prophets

Purpose/Theme:

Zephaniah preached in Judah in the seventh century, after Israel had fallen to the Assyrians. He wrote to warn both Judah and the surrounding nations of "the day of the Lord"—a future time of tribulation, but also of salvation for a faithful remnant whom God will restore to glory.

Key Verse:

"Seek the Lord, all you humble of the land, you who do what he commands. Seek righteousness, seek humility; perhaps you will be sheltered on the day of the Lord's anger" (2:3).

Outline:

☐ God's Judgment Against Judah (Zephaniah 1:1—2:3)
☐ God's Judgment Against the Nations (Zephaniah 2:4-15)
☐ The Redemption of a Remnant (Zephaniah 3)

When Events Happened

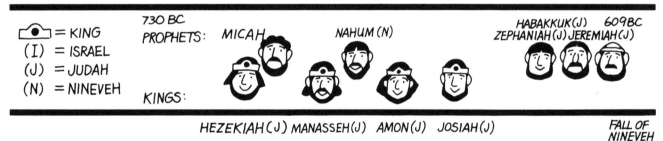

Haggai

The Books of Minor Prophets

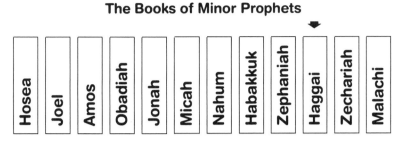

Hosea | Joel | Amos | Obadiah | Jonah | Micah | Nahum | Habakkuk | Zephaniah | Haggai | Zechariah | Malachi

Purpose/Theme:

Seventy years after being taken captive to Babylon, many Jews were allowed to return to Babylon to rebuild the Temple. Opposition from their neighbors halted the work for some fifteen years. Haggai's preaching stirred them to action and encouraged them with visions of the future glory of the Temple.

Key Verse:

"Give careful thought to your ways. You have planted much, but have harvested little . . . You earn wages, only to put them in a purse with holes in it . . . build the house, so that I may take pleasure in it and be honored" (1:5,6,8).

Outline:

☐ The Temple must be rebuilt (Haggai 1)
☐ A new Temple will be greater than the rebuilt one (Haggai 2:1-9)
☐ God's blessings will come as the Temple is rebuilt (Haggai 2:10-19)
☐ The Lord God will overthrow the nations and will bless Zerubbabel (Haggai 2:20-23)

When Events Happened

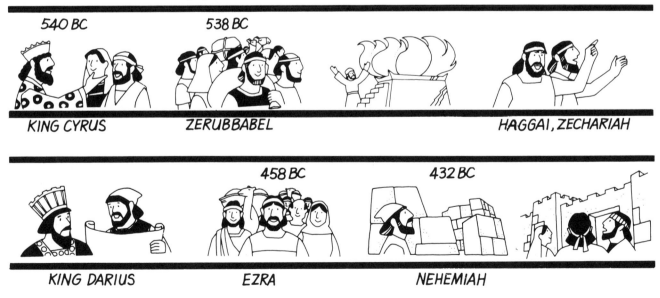

540 BC   538 BC

KING CYRUS   ZERUBBABEL   HAGGAI, ZECHARIAH

458 BC   432 BC

KING DARIUS   EZRA   NEHEMIAH

Zechariah

The Books of Minor Prophets

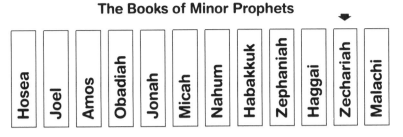

Hosea · Joel · Amos · Obadiah · Jonah · Micah · Nahum · Habakkuk · Zephaniah · Haggai · Zechariah · Malachi

Purpose/Theme:

A younger contemporary of Haggai, Zechariah also encouraged the people in the rebuilding of the Temple. His vivid visions contain many predictions of the coming of the Messiah.

Key Verse:

"Shout, Daughter of Jerusalem! See, your king comes to you, righteous and having salvation, gentle and riding on a donkey, on a colt, the foal of a donkey" (9:9).

Outline:

☐ The call to turn back to God (Zechariah 1:1-6)
☐ The eight visions of Zechariah (Zechariah 1:7—6:8)
☐ The crowning of Joshua, the high priest (Zechariah 6:9-15)
☐ The question of fasting (not eating) (Zechariah 7:1-3)
☐ The four messages of Zechariah (Zechariah 7:4—8:23)
☐ The two burdens of Zechariah (Zechariah 9—14).

When Events Happened

540 BC — KING CYRUS

538 BC — ZERUBBABEL

HAGGAI, ZECHARIAH

KING DARIUS

458 BC — EZRA

432 BC — NEHEMIAH

Malachi

The Books of Minor Prophets

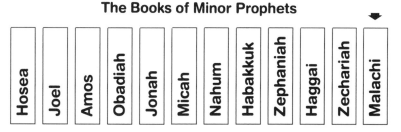

Hosea | Joel | Amos | Obadiah | Jonah | Micah | Nahum | Habakkuk | Zephaniah | Haggai | Zechariah | Malachi

Purpose/Theme:

Malachi was the last prophet of the "restoration," when the Jews were allowed to return to Jerusalem from Babylon. He explains that the woes of God's people were because of their unfaithfulness, and foresees the coming of the Messiah who would finally provide the solution to sin.

Key Verse:

"'See, I will send my messenger, who will prepare the way before me. Then suddenly the Lord you are seeking will come to his temple; the messenger of the covenant, whom you desire, will come,' says the Lord Almighty" (3:1).

Outline:

☐ God's love for the people of Israel (Malachi 1:1-5)
☐ God's complaint against the people of Israel (Malachi 1:6—2:15)
☐ The Lord's coming announced (Malachi 3:1—4:6)

When Events Happened

450 BC | 444 BC | 430 BC | 420 BC

EZRA | NEHEMIAH | MALACHI

Between the Testaments

Malachi c. 430 B.C.

From Malachi to Christ

THE PERSIAN PERIOD
450-330 B.C.

For about 200 years after Nehemiah's time the Persians controlled Judah, but the Jews were allowed to carry on their religious observances and were not interfered with. During this time Judah was ruled by high priests who were responsible to the Jewish government.

Rule of Alexander the Great

THE HELLENISTIC PERIOD
330-166 B.C.

In 333 B.C. the Persian armies stationed in Macedonia were defeated by Alexander the Great. He was convinced that Greek culture was the one force that could unify the world. Alexander permitted the Jews to observe their laws and even granted them exemption from tribute or tax during their sabbath years. When he built Alexandria in Egypt, he encouraged Jews to live there and gave them some of the same privileges he gave his Greek subjects. The Greek conquest prepared the way for the translation of the OT into Greek (Septuagint version) c. 250 B.C.

THE HASMONEAN PERIOD
166-63 B.C.

When this historical period began, the Jews were being greatly oppressed. The Ptolemies had been tolerant of the Jews and their religious practices but the Seleucid rulers were determined to force Hellenism on them. Copies of the Scriptures were ordered destroyed and laws were enforced with extreme cruelty. The oppressed Jews revolted, led by Judas the Maccabee.

THE ROMAN PERIOD
63 B.C. . . . .

In the year 63 B.C. Pompey, the Roman general, captured Jerusalem, and the provinces of Palestine became subject to Rome. The local government was entrusted part of the time to princes and the rest of the time to procurators who were appointed by the emperors. Herod the Great was ruler of all Palestine at the time of Christ's birth.

Timeline (410 – A.D. 30):

Rule of the Ptolemies of Egypt

Rule of the Seleucids of Syria

Hasmonean Dynasty

Herod the Great rules as king; subject to Rome

- 334-323 Alexander the Great conquers the East
- 330-328 Alexander's years of power
- 320 Ptolemy (I) Soter conquers Jerusalem
- 311 Seleucus conquers Babylon; Seleucid dynasty begins
- 226 Antiochus III (the Great) of Syria overpowers Palestine
- 223-187 Antiochus becomes Seleucid ruler of Syria
- 198 Antiochus defeats Egypt and gains control of Palestine
- 175-164 Antiochus (IV) Epiphanes rules Syria; Judaism is prohibited
- 167 Mattathias and his sons rebel against Antiochus; Maccabean revolt begins
- 166-160 Judas Maccabeus's leadership
- 160-143 Jonathan is high priest
- 142 Tower of Jerusalem cleansed
- 142-134 Simon becomes high priest; establishes Hasmonean dynasty
- 134-104 John Hyrcanus enlarges the independent Jewish state
- 103 Aristobulus's rule
- 102-76 Alexander Janneus's rule
- 75-67 Rule of Salome Alexandra with Hyrcanus II as high priest
- 66-63 Battle between Aristobulus II and Hyrcanus II
- 63 Pompey invades Palestine; Roman rule begins
- 63-40 Hyrcanus II rules but is subject to Rome
- 40-37 Parthians conquer Jerusalem
- 37 Jerusalem besieged for six months
- 32 Herod defeated
- 19 Herod's temple begun
- 16 Herod visits Agrippa
- 4 Herod dies; Archelaus succeeds

The New Testament Bookshelf

The term "New Testament" refers first to the covenant God made with all people to save them through His Son, Jesus Christ. It has also come to refer to the *writings about* that promise-law.

Purpose/Theme:

The Scriptures of the New Testament show how God's Old Covenant is fulfilled in Jesus Christ. It describes how the early Christians became the Church, and how to live in the light of the risen presence of Christ.

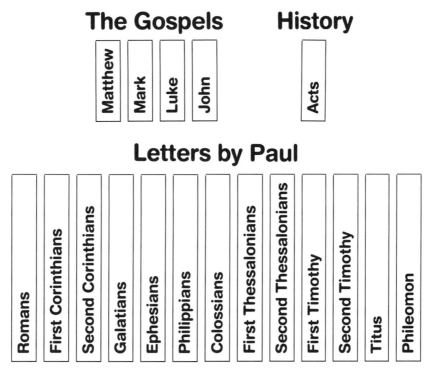

The Gospels

Matthew   Mark   Luke   John

History

Acts

Letters by Paul

Romans   First Corinthians   Second Corinthians   Galatians   Ephesians   Philippians   Colossians   First Thessalonians   Second Thessalonians   First Timothy   Second Timothy   Titus   Phileomon

General Letters

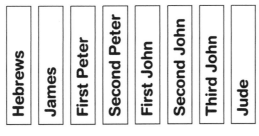

Hebrews   James   First Peter   Second Peter   First John   Second John   Third John   Jude

Prophecy

Revelation

When New Testament Events Happened

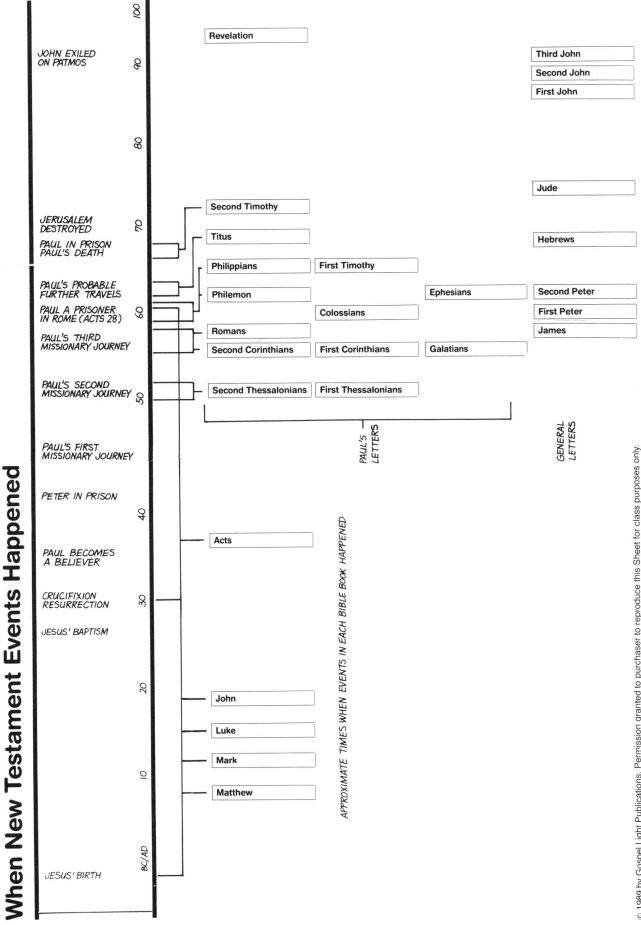

JOHN EXILED ON PATMOS	100 — Revelation
	90 — Third John / Second John / First John
	80
	Jude
JERUSALEM DESTROYED	70 — Second Timothy
PAUL IN PRISON / PAUL'S DEATH	Titus / Hebrews
PAUL'S PROBABLE FURTHER TRAVELS	Philippians / First Timothy
	Philemon / Ephesians / Second Peter
PAUL A PRISONER IN ROME (ACTS 28)	60 — Colossians / First Peter
PAUL'S THIRD MISSIONARY JOURNEY	Romans / James
	Second Corinthians / First Corinthians / Galatians
PAUL'S SECOND MISSIONARY JOURNEY	50 — Second Thessalonians / First Thessalonians
PAUL'S FIRST MISSIONARY JOURNEY	
PETER IN PRISON	
	40
PAUL BECOMES A BELIEVER	Acts
CRUCIFIXION / RESURRECTION	30
JESUS' BAPTISM	
	20 — John
	Luke
	10 — Mark
	Matthew
	BC/AD
JESUS' BIRTH	

PAUL'S LETTERS

GENERAL LETTERS

APPROXIMATE TIMES WHEN EVENTS IN EACH BIBLE BOOK HAPPENED

The Life of Christ

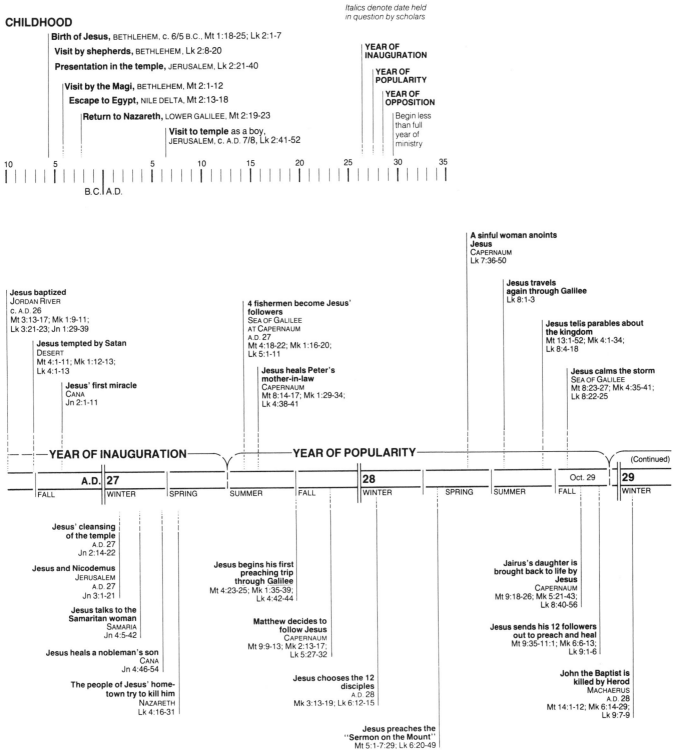

CHILDHOOD

Italics denote date held in question by scholars

Birth of Jesus, BETHLEHEM, c. 6/5 B.C., Mt 1:18-25; Lk 2:1-7

Visit by shepherds, BETHLEHEM, Lk 2:8-20

Presentation in the temple, JERUSALEM, Lk 2:21-40

Visit by the Magi, BETHLEHEM, Mt 2:1-12

Escape to Egypt, NILE DELTA, Mt 2:13-18

Return to Nazareth, LOWER GALILEE, Mt 2:19-23

Visit to temple as a boy, JERUSALEM, c. A.D. 7/8, Lk 2:41-52

YEAR OF INAUGURATION

YEAR OF POPULARITY

YEAR OF OPPOSITION
Begin less than full year of ministry

10   5   5   10   15   20   25   30   35

B.C. | A.D.

A sinful woman anoints Jesus
CAPERNAUM
Lk 7:36-50

Jesus travels again through Galilee
Lk 8:1-3

Jesus tells parables about the kingdom
Mt 13:1-52; Mk 4:1-34; Lk 8:4-18

Jesus baptized
JORDAN RIVER
c. A.D. 26
Mt 3:13-17; Mk 1:9-11;
Lk 3:21-23; Jn 1:29-39

4 fishermen become Jesus' followers
SEA OF GALILEE
AT CAPERNAUM
A.D. 27
Mt 4:18-22; Mk 1:16-20;
Lk 5:1-11

Jesus calms the storm
SEA OF GALILEE
Mt 8:23-27; Mk 4:35-41;
Lk 8:22-25

Jesus tempted by Satan
DESERT
Mt 4:1-11; Mk 1:12-13;
Lk 4:1-13

Jesus heals Peter's mother-in-law
CAPERNAUM
Mt 8:14-17; Mk 1:29-34;
Lk 4:38-41

Jesus' first miracle
CANA
Jn 2:1-11

YEAR OF INAUGURATION

YEAR OF POPULARITY

(Continued)

A.D. 27 | **28** | Oct. 29 | **29**

FALL | WINTER | SPRING | SUMMER | FALL | WINTER | SPRING | SUMMER | FALL | WINTER

Jesus' cleansing of the temple
A.D. 27
Jn 2:14-22

Jesus and Nicodemus
JERUSALEM
A.D. 27
Jn 3:1-21

Jesus talks to the Samaritan woman
SAMARIA
Jn 4:5-42

Jesus heals a nobleman's son
CANA
Jn 4:46-54

The people of Jesus' home-town try to kill him
NAZARETH
Lk 4:16-31

Jesus begins his first preaching trip through Galilee
Mt 4:23-25; Mk 1:35-39;
Lk 4:42-44

Matthew decides to follow Jesus
CAPERNAUM
Mt 9:9-13; Mk 2:13-17;
Lk 5:27-32

Jesus chooses the 12 disciples
A.D. 28
Mk 3:13-19; Lk 6:12-15

Jesus preaches the "Sermon on the Mount"
Mt 5:1-7:29; Lk 6:20-49

Jairus's daughter is brought back to life by Jesus
CAPERNAUM
Mt 9:18-26; Mk 5:21-43;
Lk 8:40-56

Jesus sends his 12 followers out to preach and heal
Mt 9:35-11:1; Mk 6:6-13;
Lk 9:1-6

John the Baptist is killed by Herod
MACHAERUS
A.D. 28
Mt 14:1-12; Mk 6:14-29;
Lk 9:7-9

Dotted lines leading to the timeline
are meant to define sequence of events only.
Exact dates, even year dates, are generally unknown.

The Life of Christ
(Continued)

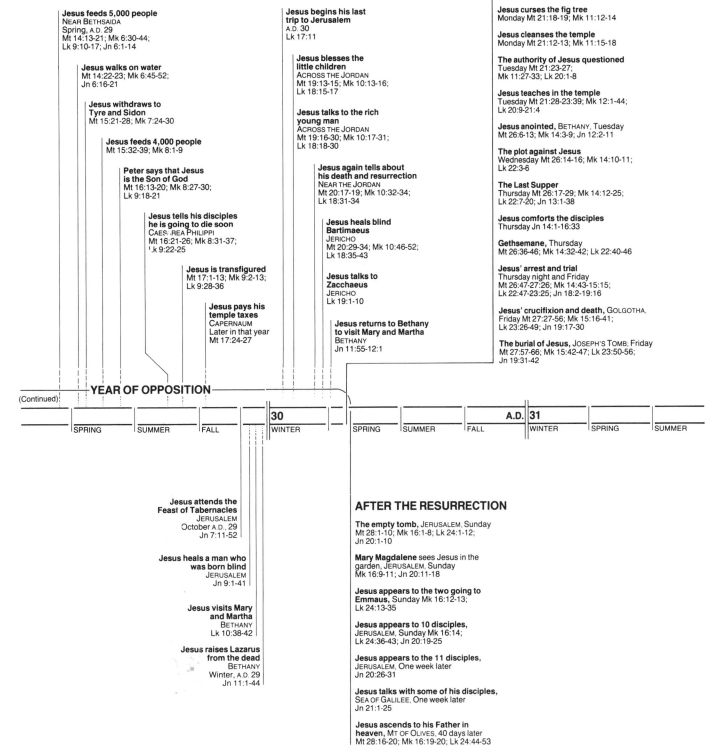

Jesus feeds 5,000 people
NEAR BETHSAIDA
Spring, A.D. 29
Mt 14:13-21; Mk 6:30-44;
Lk 9:10-17; Jn 6:1-14

Jesus walks on water
Mt 14:22-23; Mk 6:45-52;
Jn 6:16-21

**Jesus withdraws to
Tyre and Sidon**
Mt 15:21-28; Mk 7:24-30

Jesus feeds 4,000 people
Mt 15:32-39; Mk 8:1-9

**Peter says that Jesus
is the Son of God**
Mt 16:13-20; Mk 8:27-30;
Lk 9:18-21

**Jesus tells his disciples
he is going to die soon**
CAESAREA PHILIPPI
Mt 16:21-26; Mk 8:31-37;
Lk 9:22-25

Jesus is transfigured
Mt 17:1-13; Mk 9:2-13;
Lk 9:28-36

**Jesus pays his
temple taxes**
CAPERNAUM
Later in that year
Mt 17:24-27

**Jesus begins his last
trip to Jerusalem**
A.D. 30
Lk 17:11

**Jesus blesses the
little children**
ACROSS THE JORDAN
Mt 19:13-15; Mk 10:13-16;
Lk 18:15-17

**Jesus talks to the rich
young man**
ACROSS THE JORDAN
Mt 19:16-30; Mk 10:17-31;
Lk 18:18-30

**Jesus again tells about
his death and resurrection**
NEAR THE JORDAN
Mt 20:17-19; Mk 10:32-34;
Lk 18:31-34

**Jesus heals blind
Bartimaeus**
JERICHO
Mt 20:29-34; Mk 10:46-52;
Lk 18:35-43

**Jesus talks to
Zacchaeus**
JERICHO
Lk 19:1-10

**Jesus returns to Bethany
to visit Mary and Martha**
BETHANY
Jn 11:55-12:1

THE LAST WEEK

The Triumphal Entry, JERUSALEM, Sunday
Mt 21:1-11; Mk 11:1-10; Lk 19:29-44;
Jn 12:12-19

Jesus curses the fig tree
Monday Mt 21:18-19; Mk 11:12-14

Jesus cleanses the temple
Monday Mt 21:12-13; Mk 11:15-18

The authority of Jesus questioned
Tuesday Mt 21:23-27;
Mk 11:27-33; Lk 20:1-8

Jesus teaches in the temple
Tuesday Mt 21:28-23:39; Mk 12:1-44;
Lk 20:9-21:4

Jesus anointed, BETHANY, Tuesday
Mt 26:6-13; Mk 14:3-9; Jn 12:2-11

The plot against Jesus
Wednesday Mt 26:14-16; Mk 14:10-11;
Lk 22:3-6

The Last Supper
Thursday Mt 26:17-29; Mk 14:12-25;
Lk 22:7-20; Jn 13:1-38

Jesus comforts the disciples
Thursday Jn 14:1-16:33

Gethsemane, Thursday
Mt 26:36-46; Mk 14:32-42; Lk 22:40-46

Jesus' arrest and trial
Thursday night and Friday
Mt 26:47-27:26; Mk 14:43-15:15;
Lk 22:47-23:25; Jn 18:2-19:16

Jesus' crucifixion and death, GOLGOTHA,
Friday Mt 27:27-56; Mk 15:16-41;
Lk 23:26-49; Jn 19:17-30

The burial of Jesus, JOSEPH'S TOMB; Friday
Mt 27:57-66; Mk 15:42-47; Lk 23:50-56;
Jn 19:31-42

YEAR OF OPPOSITION

(Continued)

| SPRING | SUMMER | FALL | **30** WINTER | SPRING | SUMMER | FALL | A.D. **31** WINTER | SPRING | SUMMER |

**Jesus attends the
Feast of Tabernacles**
JERUSALEM
October A.D. 29
Jn 7:11-52

**Jesus heals a man who
was born blind**
JERUSALEM
Jn 9:1-41

**Jesus visits Mary
and Martha**
BETHANY
Lk 10:38-42

**Jesus raises Lazarus
from the dead**
BETHANY
Winter, A.D. 29
Jn 11:1-44

AFTER THE RESURRECTION

The empty tomb, JERUSALEM, Sunday
Mt 28:1-10; Mk 16:1-8; Lk 24:1-12;
Jn 20:1-10

Mary Magdalene sees Jesus in the
garden, JERUSALEM, Sunday
Mk 16:9-11; Jn 20:11-18

**Jesus appears to the two going to
Emmaus,** Sunday Mk 16:12-13;
Lk 24:13-35

Jesus appears to 10 disciples,
JERUSALEM, Sunday Mk 16:14;
Lk 24:36-43; Jn 20:19-25

Jesus appears to the 11 disciples,
JERUSALEM, One week later
Jn 20:26-31

Jesus talks with some of his disciples,
SEA OF GALILEE, One week later
Jn 21:1-25

**Jesus ascends to his Father in
heaven,** MT OF OLIVES, 40 days later
Mt 28:16-20; Mk 16:19-20; Lk 24:44-53

Dotted lines leading to the timeline
are meant to define sequence of events only.
Exact dates, even year dates, are generally unknown.

The Gospels

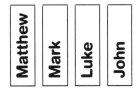

The term "gospel" comes from the Old English term "God-spell." It translates the Greek word for "good news."

One of the oldest uses of the word in the ancient world was by a king's herald, who announced the "glad tidings" of the king's birthday as he went through the cities of the realm.

This is just the meaning in our New Testaments. The four Gospels announce the glad tidings about Jesus.

The ancient world knew about history, poetry, prophecy and letters. But a "gospel" was new to them. Here, inspired writers wanted to do more than just relate historical detail. They also wanted to create faith (see John 20:30-31). They announced the good news that, just as the Old Testament had promised, God had sent His Messiah, Jesus, to the world.

Why are there *four* Gospels? Perhaps for the same reason different descriptions of a finely cut jewel would appeal to different people. *Matthew* describes one facet of the life of Christ, *Mark* another, and *Luke* a third.

These three Gospels are so much alike that they are called the *Synoptic* ("see with," or "see alike") Gospels. They all look at the life of Christ from a historical perspective. On the other hand, John's Gospel dwells more on the inner meaning of Jesus' life and teachings.

When Events Happened

Matthew

The Gospels

Purpose/Theme:

Matthew dwells especially on how the life and ministry of Jesus show Him to be the Messiah, the fulfillment of Old Testament prophecy. This Gospel is therefore often called the Gospel to the Jews.

Key Verse:

"All this took place to fulfill what the Lord had said through the prophet: 'The virgin will be with child and will give birth to a son, and they will call him Immanuel'—which means 'God with us'" (1:23).

Outline:

☐ Jesus' birth and boyhood (Matthew 1,2)
☐ Jesus' teaching and healing ministry (Matthew 3—20)
☐ Jesus' crucifixion and resurrection (Matthew 21—28)

When Events Happened

House of Herod

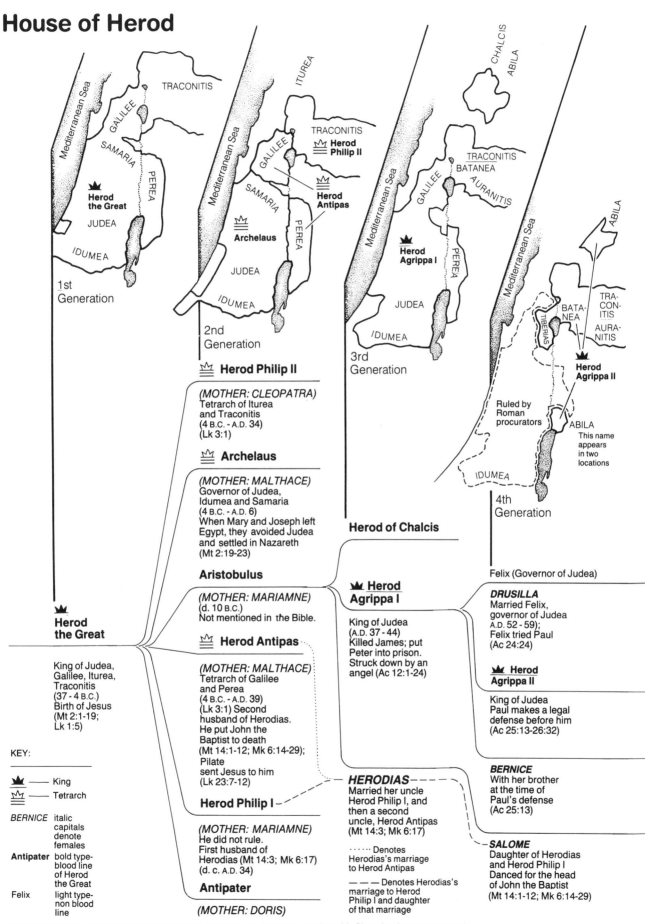

Herod Philip II

(MOTHER: CLEOPATRA)
Tetrarch of Iturea
and Traconitis
(4 B.C. - A.D. 34)
(Lk 3:1)

Archelaus

(MOTHER: MALTHACE)
Governor of Judea,
Idumea and Samaria
(4 B.C. - A.D. 6)
When Mary and Joseph left
Egypt, they avoided Judea
and settled in Nazareth
(Mt 2:19-23)

Aristobulus

(MOTHER: MARIAMNE)
(d. 10 B.C.)
Not mentioned in the Bible.

Herod Antipas

(MOTHER: MALTHACE)
Tetrarch of Galilee
and Perea
(4 B.C. - A.D. 39)
(Lk 3:1) Second
husband of Herodias.
He put John the
Baptist to death
(Mt 14:1-12; Mk 6:14-29);
Pilate
sent Jesus to him
(Lk 23:7-12)

Herod Philip I

(MOTHER: MARIAMNE)
He did not rule.
First husband of
Herodias (Mt 14:3; Mk 6:17)
(d. c. A.D. 34)

Antipater

(MOTHER: DORIS)

Herod the Great

King of Judea,
Galilee, Iturea,
Traconitis
(37 - 4 B.C.)
Birth of Jesus
(Mt 2:1-19;
Lk 1:5)

Herod of Chalcis

Herod Agrippa I

King of Judea
(A.D. 37 - 44)
Killed James; put
Peter into prison.
Struck down by an
angel (Ac 12:1-24)

HERODIAS
Married her uncle
Herod Philip I, and
then a second
uncle, Herod Antipas
(Mt 14:3; Mk 6:17)

Felix (Governor of Judea)

DRUSILLA
Married Felix,
governor of Judea
A.D. 52 - 59);
Felix tried Paul
(Ac 24:24)

Herod Agrippa II

King of Judea
Paul makes a legal
defense before him
(Ac 25:13-26:32)

BERNICE
With her brother
at the time of
Paul's defense
(Ac 25:13)

SALOME
Daughter of Herodias
and Herod Philip I
Danced for the head
of John the Baptist
(Mt 14:1-12; Mk 6:14-29)

KEY:

⚜ —— King

⚜ —— Tetrarch

BERNICE italic
         capitals
         denote
         females

Antipater bold type-
               blood line
               of Herod
               the Great

Felix light type-
       non blood
       line

······ Denotes
Herodias's marriage
to Herod Antipas

— — — Denotes Herodias's
marriage to Herod
Philip I and daughter
of that marriage

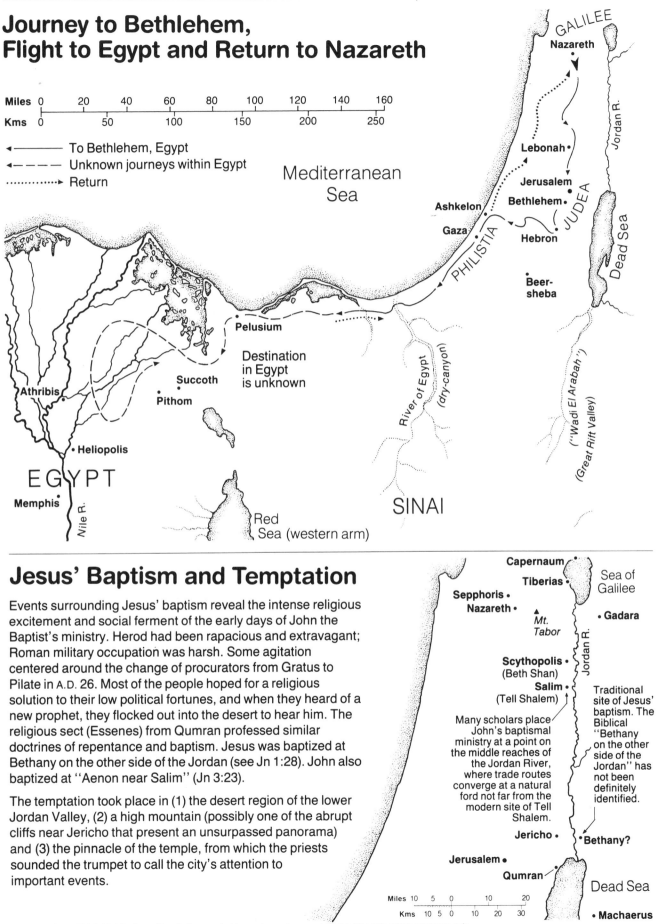

Journey to Bethlehem, Flight to Egypt and Return to Nazareth

| Miles | 0 | 20 | 40 | 60 | 80 | 100 | 120 | 140 | 160 |

| Kms | 0 | 50 | 100 | 150 | 200 | 250 |

◄——————— To Bethlehem, Egypt
◄— — — — Unknown journeys within Egypt
············► Return

GALILEE
Nazareth

Mediterranean
Sea

Lebonah

Jerusalem
Bethlehem   JUDEA
Ashkelon
Gaza   Hebron
PHILISTIA

Dead Sea

Jordan R.

Beer-
sheba

Pelusium

Destination
in Egypt
is unknown

Succoth
Pithom

River of Egypt
(dry-canyon)

("Wadi El Arabah")
(Great Rift Valley)

Athribis

Heliopolis

EGYPT

Memphis

Nile R.

SINAI

Red
Sea (western arm)

Jesus' Baptism and Temptation

Events surrounding Jesus' baptism reveal the intense religious excitement and social ferment of the early days of John the Baptist's ministry. Herod had been rapacious and extravagant; Roman military occupation was harsh. Some agitation centered around the change of procurators from Gratus to Pilate in A.D. 26. Most of the people hoped for a religious solution to their low political fortunes, and when they heard of a new prophet, they flocked out into the desert to hear him. The religious sect (Essenes) from Qumran professed similar doctrines of repentance and baptism. Jesus was baptized at Bethany on the other side of the Jordan (see Jn 1:28). John also baptized at "Aenon near Salim" (Jn 3:23).

The temptation took place in (1) the desert region of the lower Jordan Valley, (2) a high mountain (possibly one of the abrupt cliffs near Jericho that present an unsurpassed panorama) and (3) the pinnacle of the temple, from which the priests sounded the trumpet to call the city's attention to important events.

Capernaum
Tiberias   Sea of
                        Galilee
Sepphoris
Nazareth   Mt.   • Gadara
                 Tabor

                 Jordan R.

Scythopolis
(Beth Shan)
Salim
(Tell Shalem)   Traditional
                               site of Jesus'
Many scholars place   baptism. The
John's baptismal   Biblical
ministry at a point on   "Bethany
the middle reaches of   on the other
the Jordan River,   side of the
where trade routes   Jordan" has
converge at a natural   not been
ford not far from the   definitely
modern site of Tell   identified.
Shalem.

Jericho   • Bethany?

Jerusalem •

Qumran   Dead Sea

| Miles | 10 | 5 | 0 | 10 | 20 |
| Kms | 10 | 5 | 0 | 10 | 20 | 30 |

• Machaerus

Herod's Temple

20 B.C.—A.D. 70

Begun in 20 B.C., Herod's new structure towered 15 stories high, following the floor dimensions of the former temples in the Holy Place and the Most Holy Place. The high sanctuary shown here in a cutaway view was built on the site of the former temples of Solomon and Zerubbabel, and was completed in just 18 months.

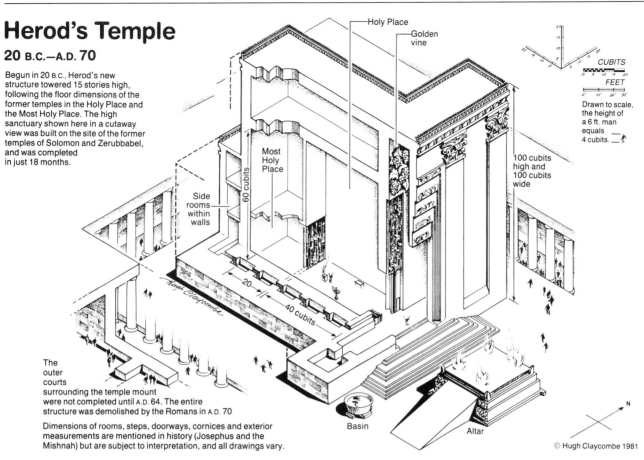

The outer courts surrounding the temple mount were not completed until A.D. 64. The entire structure was demolished by the Romans in A.D. 70

Dimensions of rooms, steps, doorways, cornices and exterior measurements are mentioned in history (Josephus and the Mishnah) but are subject to interpretation, and all drawings vary.

© Hugh Claycombe 1981

Jewish Sects

PHARISEES

Their roots can be traced to the second century B.C.—to the Hasidim.

1. Along with the Torah, they accepted as equally inspired and authoritative, all material contained within the oral tradition.
2. On free will and determination, they held to a mediating view that made it impossible for either free will or the sovereignty of God to cancel out the other.
3. They accepted a rather developed hierarchy of angels and demons.
4. They taught that there was a future for the dead.
5. They believed in the immortality of the soul and in reward and retribution after death.
6. They were champions of human equality.
7. The emphasis of their teaching was ethical rather than theological.

SADDUCEES

They probably had their beginning during the Hasmonean period (166-63 B.C.). Their demise occurred c. A.D. 70 with the fall of Jerusalem.

1. They denied that the oral law was authoritative and binding.
2. They interpreted Mosaic law more literally than did the Pharisees.
3. They were very exacting in Levitical purity.
4. They attributed all to free will.
5. They argued there is neither resurrection of the dead nor a future life.
6. They rejected a belief in angels and demons.
7. They rejected the idea of a spiritual world.
8. Only the books of Moses were canonical Scripture.

ESSENES

They probably originated among the Hasidim, along with the Pharisees, from whom they later separated (I Maccabees 2:42; 7:13). They were a group of very strict and zealous Jews who took part with the Maccabeans in a revolt against the Syrians, c. 165-155 B.C.

1. They followed a strict observance of the purity laws of the Torah.
2. They were notable for their communal ownership of property.
3. They had a strong sense of mutual responsibility.
4. Daily worship was an important feature along with a daily study of their sacred scriptures.
5. Solemn oaths of piety and obedience had to be taken.
6. Sacrifices were offered on holy days and during sacred seasons.
7. Marriage was not condemned in principle but was avoided.
8. They attributed all that happened to fate.

ZEALOTS

They originated during the reign of Herod the Great c. 6 B.C. and ceased to exist in A.D. 73 at Masada.

1. They opposed payment of tribute for taxes to a pagan emperor, saying that allegiance was due only to God.
2. They held a fierce loyalty to the Jewish traditions.
3. They were opposed to the use of the Greek language in Palestine.
4. They prophesied the coming of the time of salvation.

Mark
The Gospels
▼

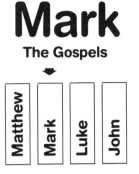

Purpose/Theme:
Mark's overall picture of the life of Christ is more complete than the other Gospels, even though it is more concise, and therefore the shortest. Mark emphasizes the larger-than-life, wonderous nature of Jesus. Since many Romans in the ancient world were attracted to such powerful portrayals, Mark is often called the Gospel to the Romans.

Key Verse:
"Jesus went into Galilee, proclaiming the good news of God. 'The time has come,' he said. 'The kingdom of God is near. Repent and believe the good news!'" (1:14,15).

Outline:
☐ Jesus, the Servant—serving people (Mark 1—10)
☐ Jesus, the Servant—giving His life to save others (Mark 11—16)

When Events Happened

Decapolis and the Lands Beyond Jordan

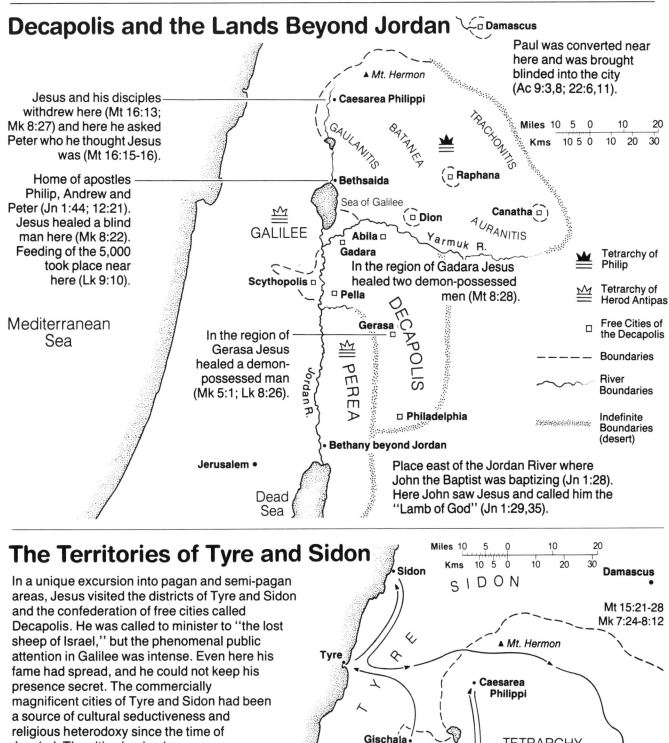

Paul was converted near here and was brought blinded into the city (Ac 9:3,8; 22:6,11).

Jesus and his disciples withdrew here (Mt 16:13; Mk 8:27) and here he asked Peter who he thought Jesus was (Mt 16:15-16).

Home of apostles Philip, Andrew and Peter (Jn 1:44; 12:21). Jesus healed a blind man here (Mk 8:22). Feeding of the 5,000 took place near here (Lk 9:10).

In the region of Gadara Jesus healed two demon-possessed men (Mt 8:28).

In the region of Gerasa Jesus healed a demon-possessed man (Mk 5:1; Lk 8:26).

Place east of the Jordan River where John the Baptist was baptizing (Jn 1:28). Here John saw Jesus and called him the "Lamb of God" (Jn 1:29,35).

Tetrarchy of Philip

Tetrarchy of Herod Antipas

Free Cities of the Decapolis

Boundaries

River Boundaries

Indefinite Boundaries (desert)

The Territories of Tyre and Sidon

In a unique excursion into pagan and semi-pagan areas, Jesus visited the districts of Tyre and Sidon and the confederation of free cities called Decapolis. He was called to minister to "the lost sheep of Israel," but the phenomenal public attention in Galilee was intense. Even here his fame had spread, and he could not keep his presence secret. The commercially magnificent cities of Tyre and Sidon had been a source of cultural seductiveness and religious heterodoxy since the time of Jezebel. The cities having been heavily influenced by Hellenism, the sophistication of Greek culture was apparent in their coinage and architecture. Each was also a proud, historic center of Canaanite paganism, with tombs of ancient kings and temples to Melqart/Heracles, Astarte and various other deities.

Mt 15:21-28
Mk 7:24-8:12

Jerusalem
During the Ministry of Jesus

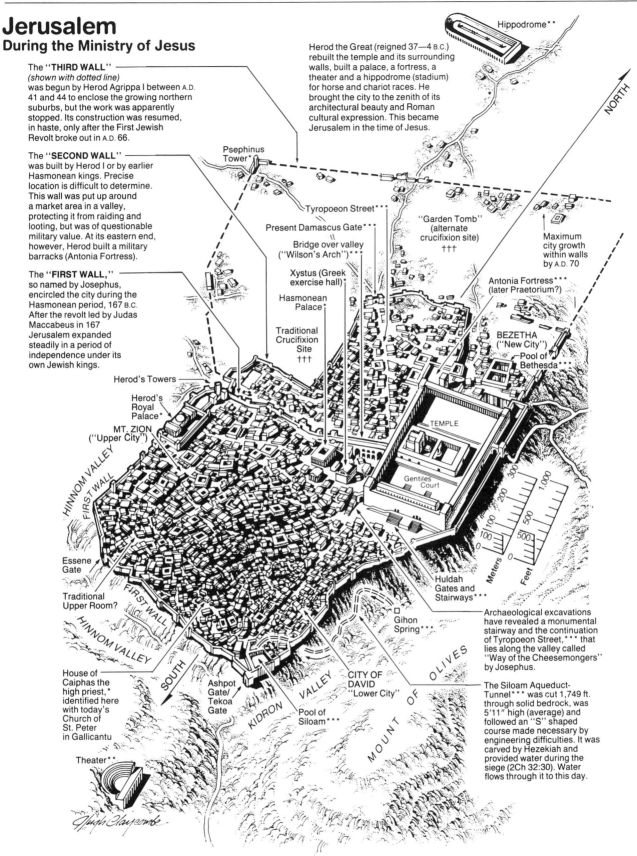

The "**THIRD WALL**" ——
(shown with dotted line)
was begun by Herod Agrippa I between A.D. 41 and 44 to enclose the growing northern suburbs, but the work was apparently stopped. Its construction was resumed, in haste, only after the First Jewish Revolt broke out in A.D. 66.

The "**SECOND WALL**" ——
was built by Herod I or by earlier Hasmonean kings. Precise location is difficult to determine. This wall was put up around a market area in a valley, protecting it from raiding and looting, but was of questionable military value. At its eastern end, however, Herod built a military barracks (Antonia Fortress).

The "**FIRST WALL**," ——
so named by Josephus, encircled the city during the Hasmonean period, 167 B.C. After the revolt led by Judas Maccabeus in 167 Jerusalem expanded steadily in a period of independence under its own Jewish kings.

Herod the Great (reigned 37—4 B.C.) rebuilt the temple and its surrounding walls, built a palace, a fortress, a theater and a hippodrome (stadium) for horse and chariot races. He brought the city to the zenith of its architectural beauty and Roman cultural expression. This became Jerusalem in the time of Jesus.

Hippodrome**

NORTH

Psephinus Tower*

Tyropoeon Street***

Present Damascus Gate***

Bridge over valley ("Wilson's Arch")***

Xystus (Greek exercise hall)*

Hasmonean Palace*

Traditional Crucifixion Site †††

"Garden Tomb" (alternate crucifixion site) †††

Maximum city growth within walls by A.D. 70

Antonia Fortress*** (later Praetorium?)

BEZETHA ("New City")

Pool of Bethesda***

Herod's Towers

Herod's Royal Palace*

MT. ZION ("Upper City")

HINNOM VALLEY

FIRST WALL

TEMPLE

Gentiles Court

300
200
100

1,000
500

Meters

Feet

Essene Gate

Traditional Upper Room?

FIRST WALL

HINNOM VALLEY

SOUTH

House of Caiphas the high priest,* identified here with today's Church of St. Peter in Gallicantu

Ashpot Gate/ Tekoa Gate

Pool of Siloam***

KIDRON VALLEY

CITY OF DAVID "Lower City"

Gihon Spring***

Huldah Gates and Stairways***

MOUNT OF OLIVES

Theater**

Archaeological excavations have revealed a monumental stairway and the continuation of Tyropoeon Street,*** that lies along the valley called "Way of the Cheesemongers" by Josephus.

The Siloam Aqueduct-Tunnel*** was cut 1,749 ft. through solid bedrock, was 5'11" high (average) and followed an "S" shaped course made necessary by engineering difficulties. It was carved by Hezekiah and provided water during the siege (2Ch 32:30). Water flows through it to this day.

* Location generally known, but style of architecture is unknown; artist's concept only, and Roman architecture is assumed.

** Location and architecture unknown, but referred to in written history; shown here for illustrative purposes.

*** Ancient feature has remained, or appearance has been determined from evidence.

Buildings, streets and roads shown here are artist's concept only unless otherwise named and located. Wall heights remain generally unknown, except for those surrounding the Temple Mount.

DEEP VALLEYS on the east, south and west permitted urban expansion only to the north.

© Hugh Claycombe 1982

Passion Week

Bethany, the Mount of Olives and Jerusalem

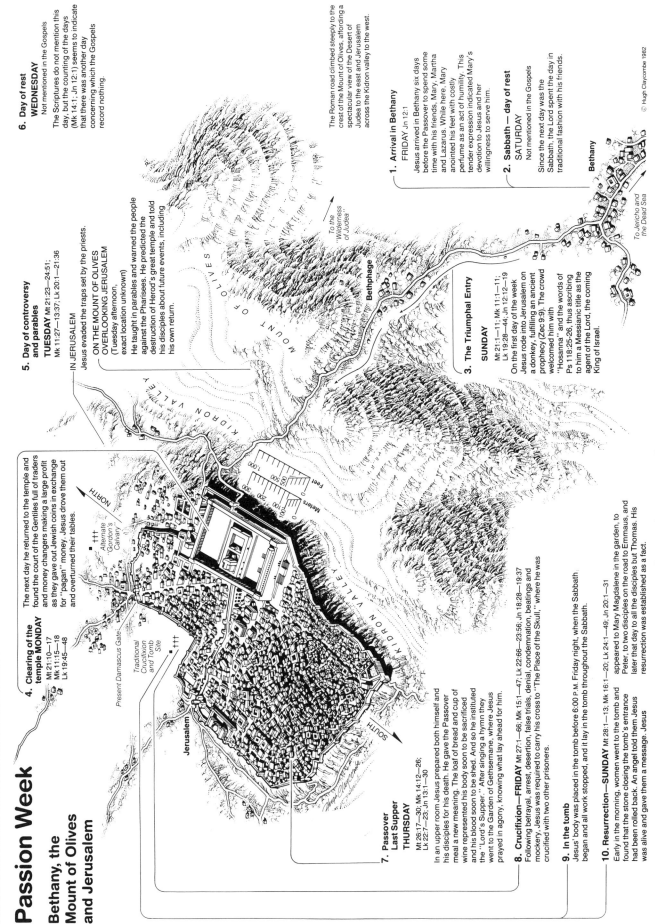

6. Day of rest
WEDNESDAY

Not mentioned in the Gospels

The Scriptures do not mention this day, but the counting of the days (Mk 14:1; Jn 12:1) seems to indicate that there was another day concerning which the Gospels record nothing.

The Roman road climbed steeply to the crest of the Mount of Olives, affording a spectacular view of the Desert of Judea to the east and Jerusalem across the Kidron valley to the west.

1. Arrival in Bethany
FRIDAY Jn 12:1

Jesus arrived in Bethany six days before the Passover to spend some time with his friends, Mary, Martha and Lazarus. While here, Mary anointed his feet with costly perfume as an act of humility. This tender expression indicated Mary's devotion to Jesus and her willingness to serve him.

2. Sabbath — day of rest
SATURDAY

Not mentioned in the Gospels

Since the next day was the Sabbath, the Lord spent the day in traditional fashion with his friends.

5. Day of controversy and parables
TUESDAY Mt 21:23—24:51; Mk 11:27—13:37; Lk 20:1—21:36

IN JERUSALEM

Jesus evaded the traps set by the priests.

ON THE MOUNT OF OLIVES OVERLOOKING JERUSALEM (Tuesday afternoon, exact location unknown)

He taught in parables and warned the people against the Pharisees. He predicted the destruction of Herod's great temple and told his disciples about future events, including his own return.

3. The Triumphal Entry
SUNDAY

Mt 21:1—11; Mk 11:1—11; Lk 19:28—44; Jn 12:12—19

On the first day of the week Jesus rode into Jerusalem on a donkey, fulfilling an ancient prophecy (Zec 9:9). The crowd welcomed him with "Hosanna," and the words of Ps 118:25-26, thus ascribing to him a Messianic title as the agent of the Lord, the coming King of Israel.

4. Clearing of the temple MONDAY

Mt 21:10—17
Mk 11:15—18
Lk 19:45—48

The next day he returned to the temple and found the court of the Gentiles full of traders and money changers making a large profit as they gave out Jewish coins in exchange for "pagan" money. Jesus drove them out and overturned their tables.

7. Passover Last Supper THURSDAY

Mt 26:17—30; Mk 14:12—26; Lk 22:7—23; Jn 13:1—30

In an upper room Jesus prepared both himself and his disciples for his death. He gave the Passover meal a new meaning. The loaf of bread and cup of wine represented his body soon to be sacrificed and his blood soon to be shed. And so he instituted the "Lord's Supper." After singing a hymn they went to the Garden of Gethsemane, where Jesus prayed in agony, knowing what lay ahead for him.

8. Crucifixion—FRIDAY Mt 27:1—66; Mk 15:1—47; Lk 22:66—23:56; Jn 18:28—19:37

Following betrayal, arrest, desertion, false trials, denial, condemnation, beatings and mockery, Jesus was required to carry his cross to "The Place of the Skull," where he was crucified with two other prisoners.

9. In the tomb

Jesus' body was placed in the tomb before 6:00 P.M. Friday night, when the Sabbath began and all work stopped, and it lay in the tomb throughout the Sabbath.

10. Resurrection—SUNDAY Mt 28:1—13; Mk 16:1—20; Lk 24:1—49; Jn 20:1—31

Early in the morning, women went to the tomb and found that the stone closing the tomb's entrance had been rolled back. An angel told them Jesus was alive and gave them a message. Jesus appeared to Mary Magdalene in the garden, to Peter, to two disciples on the road to Emmaus, and later that day to all the disciples but Thomas. His resurrection was established as a fact.

Present Damascus Gate

Traditional Crucifixion and Tomb Site

Alternate "Gordon's Calvary"

Jerusalem

NORTH

SOUTH

Feet / Meters
1,000 / 300
500 / 200
100
0

KIDRON VALLEY

MOUNT OF OLIVES

Bethphage

Bethany

To the "Wilderness of Judea"

To Jericho and the Dead Sea

© Hugh Claycombe 1982

Luke
The Gospels

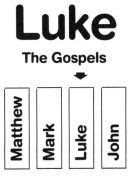

Purpose/Theme:

Luke (who also probably wrote the book of Acts) was a Greek physician. His book is often called the Gospel to the Greeks because it emphasizes the beauty of Jesus' humanity and His acceptance of gentiles, women, children and the poor—traits which the Greeks often associated with the Ideal or Universal Man.

Key Verse:

"If anyone would come after me, he must deny himself and take up his cross daily and follow me. For whoever wants to save his life will lose it, but whoever loses his life for me will save it" (9:23,24).

Outline:

☐ Jesus, the Son of Man, grows up (Luke 1—4:13)
☐ Jesus, the Son of Man, has power over everything (Luke 4:14—9:50)
☐ Jesus, the Son of Man, teaches His disciples (Luke 9:51—19:17)
☐ Jesus, the Son of Man, suffers and dies (Luke 19:28—23:56)
☐ Jesus, the Son of Man, lives again forever (Luke 24)

When Events Happened

Palestine under Herod the Great

37-4 B.C.

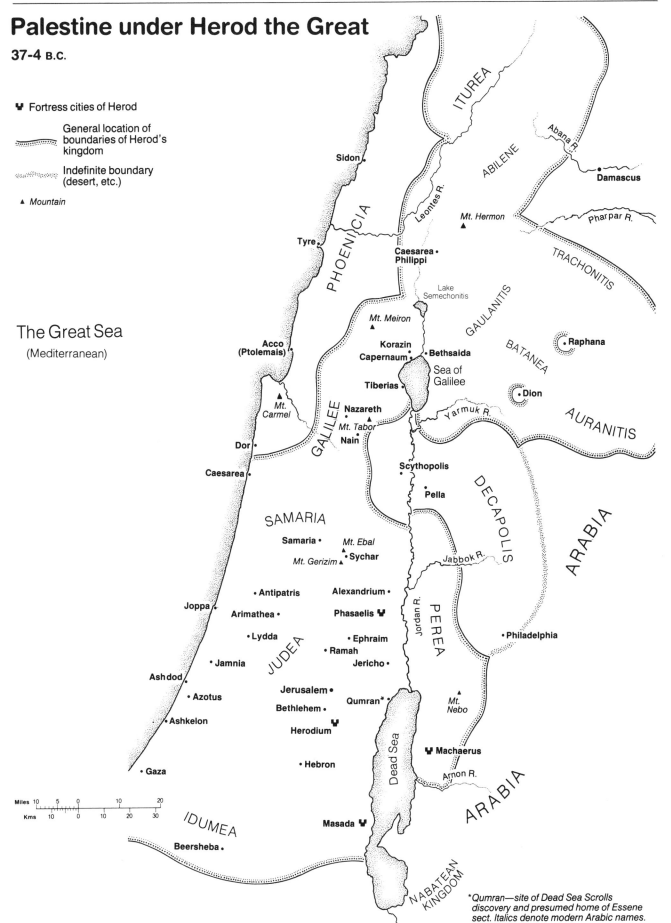

♉ Fortress cities of Herod

～ General location of boundaries of Herod's kingdom

～ Indefinite boundary (desert, etc.)

▲ *Mountain*

The Great Sea

(Mediterranean)

ITUREA

ABILENE

Abana R.

Damascus

Pharpar R.

Sidon

Leontes R.

Mt. Hermon

TRACHONITIS

Tyre

PHOENICIA

Caesarea
Philippi

Lake Semechonitis

GAULANITIS

BATANEA

Raphana

Acco
(Ptolemais)

Mt. Meiron

Korazin

Capernaum

Bethsaida

Sea of Galilee

Dion

AURANITIS

Mt. Carmel

GALILEE

Nazareth

Tiberias

Yarmuk R.

Dor

Mt. Tabor

Nain

Caesarea

Scythopolis

DECAPOLIS

ARABIA

Pella

SAMARIA

Samaria

Mt. Ebal

Mt. Gerizim ▲ Sychar

Jabbok R.

Antipatris

Alexandrium

Joppa

Arimathea

Phasaelis ♉

Jordan R.

PEREA

Philadelphia

Lydda

Ephraim

Ramah

Jericho

Jamnia

JUDEA

Ashdod

Azotus

Jerusalem

Qumran*

Mt. Nebo

Ashkelon

Bethlehem

Herodium ♉

Dead Sea

Machaerus ♉

Hebron

Arnon R.

Gaza

Miles 10 5 0   10   20

Kms   10   0   10   20   30

IDUMEA

Masada ♉

ARABIA

Beersheba

NABATEAN KINGDOM

Qumran—site of Dead Sea Scrolls discovery and presumed home of Essene sect. Italics denote modern Arabic names.

Parables of Jesus

	MATTHEW	MARK	LUKE
Lamp under a bowl	5:14-15	4:21-22	8:16; 11:33
Wise and foolish builders	7:24-27		6:47-49
New cloth on an old coat	9:16	2:21	5:36
New wine in old wineskins	9:17	2:22	5:37-38
Sower and the soils	13:3-8,18-23	4:3-8,14-20	8:5-8,11-15
Weeds	13:24-30, 36-43		
Mustard seed	13:31-32	4:30-32	13:18-19
Yeast	13:33		13:20-21
Hidden treasure	13:44		
Valuable pearl	13:45-46		
Net	13:47-50		
Owner of a house	13:52		
Lost sheep	18:12-14		15:4-7
Unmerciful servant	18:23-34		
Workers in the vineyard	20:1-16		
Two sons	21:28-32		
Tenants	21:33-44	12:1-11	20:9-18
Wedding banquet	22:2-14		
Fig tree	24:32-35	13:28-29	21:29-31
Faithful and wise servant	24:45-51		12:42-48
Ten virgins	25:1-13		
Talents (minas)	25:14-30		19:12-27
Sheep and goats	25:31-46		
Growing seed		4:26-29	
Watchful servants		13:35-37	12:35-40
Moneylender			7:41-43
Good Samaritan			10:30-37
Friend in need			11:5-8
Rich fool			12:16-21
Unfruitful fig tree			13:6-9
Lowest seat at the feast			14:7-14
Great banquet			14:16-24
Cost of discipleship			14:28-33
Lost coin			15:8-10
Lost (prodigal) son			15:11-32
Shrewd manager			16:1-8
Rich man and Lazarus			16:19-31
Master and his servant			17:7-10
Persistent widow			18:2-8
Pharisee and tax collector			18:10-14

Capernaum Synagogue

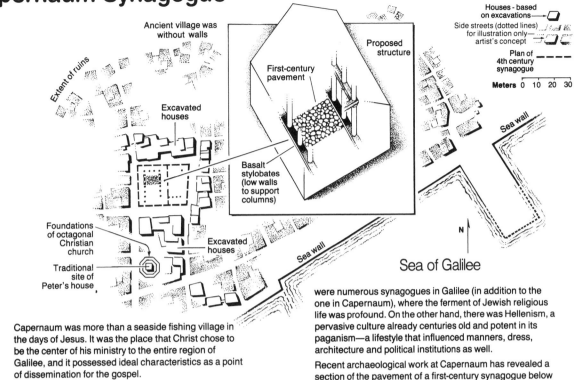

Capernaum was more than a seaside fishing village in the days of Jesus. It was the place that Christ chose to be the center of his ministry to the entire region of Galilee, and it possessed ideal characteristics as a point of dissemination for the gospel.

There were good reasons for this. The town itself was named *Kephar Nahum*, "village of (perhaps the prophet), Nahum" and was the centerpiece of a densely populated region having a bicultural flavor. On the one hand, there

were numerous synagogues in Galilee (in addition to the one in Capernaum), where the ferment of Jewish religious life was profound. On the other hand, there was Hellenism, a pervasive culture already centuries old and potent in its paganism—a lifestyle that influenced manners, dress, architecture and political institutions as well.

Recent archaeological work at Capernaum has revealed a section of the pavement of a first-century synagogue below the still-existing ruins of the fourth-century one on the site. A private house later made into a church and a place of pilgrimage has yielded some evidence that may link it to the site of Simon Peter's house (Lk 4:38).

Resurrection Appearances

EVENT	DATE	Matthew	Mark	Luke	John	Acts	I Corinthians
At the empty tomb outside Jerusalem	Early Sunday morning	28:1-10	16:1-8	24:1-12	20:1-9		
To Mary Magdalene at the tomb	Early Sunday morning		16:9-11		20:11-18		
To two travelers on the road to Emmaus	Sunday at midday			24:13-32			
To Peter in Jerusalem	During the day on Sunday			24:34			15:5
To the ten disciples in the upper room	Sunday evening		16:14	24:36-43	20:19-25		
To the eleven disciples in the upper room	One week later				20:26-31		15:5
To seven disciples fishing on the Sea of Galilee	One day at daybreak				21:1-23		
To the eleven disciples on the mountain in Galilee	Some time later	28:16-20	16:15-18				
To more than 500	Some time later						15:6
To James	Some time later						15:7
At the Ascension on the Mt. of Olives	Forty days after the resurrection			24:44-49		1:3-8	

John

The Gospels ↓

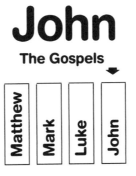

Purpose/Theme:
John says expressly that he wrote so that people might come to believe in Christ (20:30-31). He was not as interested in the historical order of the events in the life of Christ, or in His deeds, as he was in the inner meaning of His teaching. Balancing Luke's emphasis on the humanity of Jesus, John dwells on His deity.

Key Verses:
"I am the bread of life. He who comes to me will never go hungry" (6:35). "I am the resurrection and the life. He who believes in me will live" (11:25). "I am the way and the truth and the life. No one comes to the Father except through me" (14:6).

Outline:
☐ Jesus God's Son's healing and teaching ministry (John 1:1-12)
☐ Jesus God's Son's death and resurrection (John 13-21)

When Events Happened

Jesus in Judea and Samaria

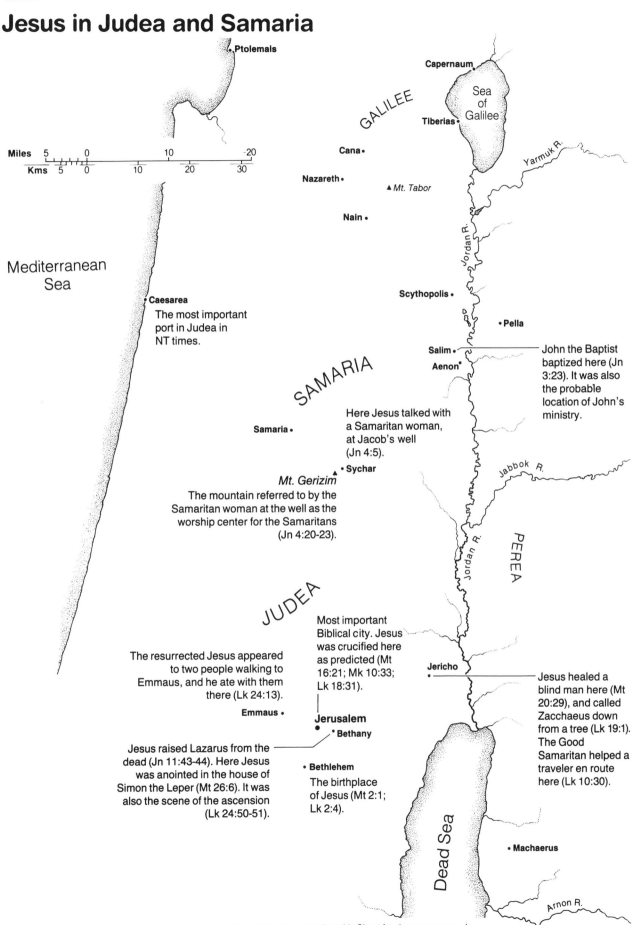

Ptolemais

GALILEE

Capernaum

Sea of Galilee

Tiberias

Cana

Nazareth

▲ Mt. Tabor

Nain

Yarmuk R.

Jordan R.

Scythopolis

Pella

Miles 5 0 10 -20
Kms 5 0 10 20 30

Mediterranean Sea

Caesarea
The most important port in Judea in NT times.

SAMARIA

Salim

Aenon

John the Baptist baptized here (Jn 3:23). It was also the probable location of John's ministry.

Here Jesus talked with a Samaritan woman, at Jacob's well (Jn 4:5).

Samaria

Sychar

Jabbok R.

Mt. Gerizim
The mountain referred to by the Samaritan woman at the well as the worship center for the Samaritans (Jn 4:20-23).

Jordan R.

PEREA

JUDEA

Most important Biblical city. Jesus was crucified here as predicted (Mt 16:21; Mk 10:33; Lk 18:31).

The resurrected Jesus appeared to two people walking to Emmaus, and he ate with them there (Lk 24:13).

Jericho

Jesus healed a blind man here (Mt 20:29), and called Zacchaeus down from a tree (Lk 19:1). The Good Samaritan helped a traveler en route here (Lk 10:30).

Emmaus

Jerusalem

Bethany

Jesus raised Lazarus from the dead (Jn 11:43-44). Here Jesus was anointed in the house of Simon the Leper (Mt 26:6). It was also the scene of the ascension (Lk 24:50-51).

Bethlehem
The birthplace of Jesus (Mt 2:1; Lk 2:4).

Dead Sea

Machaerus

Arnon R.

Jesus in Galilee

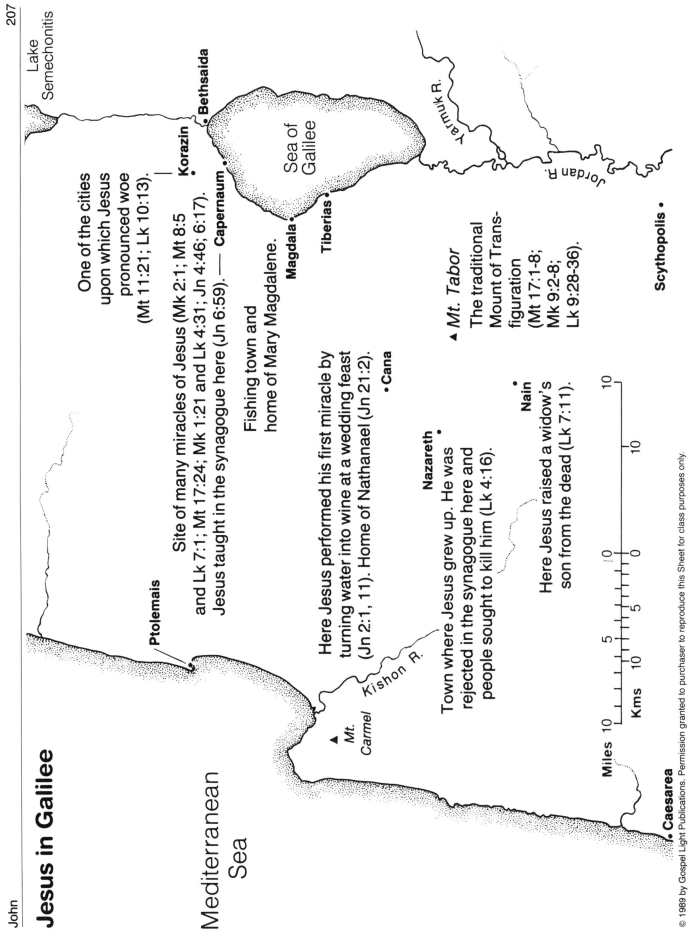

Lake Semechonitis

Mediterranean Sea

Ptolemais

One of the cities upon which Jesus pronounced woe (Mt 11:21; Lk 10:13).

Korazin

Bethsaida

Capernaum — Site of many miracles of Jesus (Mk 2:1; Mt 8:5 and Lk 7:1; Mt 17:24; Mk 1:21 and Lk 4:31; Jn 4:46; 6:17). Jesus taught in the synagogue here (Jn 6:59).

Fishing town and home of Mary Magdalene. **Magdala**

Sea of Galilee

Tiberias

Yarmuk R.

Jordan R.

Scythopolis

▲ *Mt. Tabor* The traditional Mount of Transfiguration (Mt 17:1-8; Mk 9:2-8; Lk 9:28-36).

•**Cana**

Here Jesus performed his first miracle by turning water into wine at a wedding feast (Jn 2:1, 11). Home of Nathanael (Jn 21:2).

Nazareth Town where Jesus grew up. He was rejected in the synagogue here and people sought to kill him (Lk 4:16).

Nain Here Jesus raised a widow's son from the dead (Lk 7:11).

▲ *Mt. Carmel*

Kishon R.

Miles 10   5   0   5   10

Kms 10   5   0   10   10

•**Caesarea**

Miracles of Jesus

Healing	MATTHEW	MARK	LUKE	JOHN
Man with leprosy	8:2-4	1:40-42	5:12-13	
Roman centurion's servant	8:5-13		7:1-10	
Peter's mother-in-law	8:14-15	1:30-31	4:38-39	
Two men from Gadara	8:28-34	5:1-15	8:27-35	
Paralyzed man	9:2-7	2:3-12	5:18-25	
Woman with bleeding	9:20-22	5:25-29	8:43-48	
Two blind men	9:27-31			
Man mute and possessed	9:32-33			
Man with a shriveled hand	12:10-13	3:1-5	6:6-10	
Man blind, mute and possessed	12:22		11:14	
Canaanite woman's daughter	15:21-28	7:24-30		
Boy with a demon	17:14-18	9:17-29	9:38-43	
Two blind men (one named)	20:29-34	10:46-52	18:35-43	
Deaf mute		7:31-37		
Man possessed, synagogue		1:23-26	4:33-35	
Blind man at Bethsaida		8:22-26		
Crippled woman			13:11-13	
Man with dropsy			14:1-4	
Ten men with leprosy			17:11-19	
The high priest's servant			22:50-51	
Official's son at Capernaum				4:46-54
Sick man, pool of Bethesda				5:1-9
Man born blind				9:1-7

Command over the forces of nature	MATTHEW	MARK	LUKE	JOHN
Calming the storm	8:23-27	4:37-41	8:22-25	
Walking on the water	14:25	6:48-51		6:19-21
5,000 people fed	14:15-21	6:35-44	9:12-17	6:5-13
4,000 people fed	15:32-38	8:1-9		
Coin in the fish's mouth	17:24-27			
Fig tree withered	21:18-22	11:12-14, 20-25		
Catch of fish			5:4-11	
Water turned into wine				2:1-11
Another catch of fish				21:1-11

Bringing the dead back to life	MATTHEW	MARK	LUKE	JOHN
Jairus's daughter	9:18-19, 23-25	5:22-24, 38-42	8:41-42, 49-56	
Widow's son at Nain			7:11-15	
Lazarus				11:1-44

History

Acts

The book of Acts is the only book of history in the New Testament—compared with 12 in the Old Testament.

But the fact that the New Testament includes a book of history is very important. It means that New Testament faith, like that of the Old Testament, is tied to actual events. The myths that were the basis of pagan religions were growing old at the time of the New Testament. At just the right time, the earliest Christians could say, "Listen to us—here is something that actually happened in the full light of history!"

A good way to start reading Acts is to read the last chapter of Luke and the first chapter of Acts at the same setting. Many scholars believe that Luke wrote Acts as a kind of "Book II" to follow his Gospel.

When Events Happened

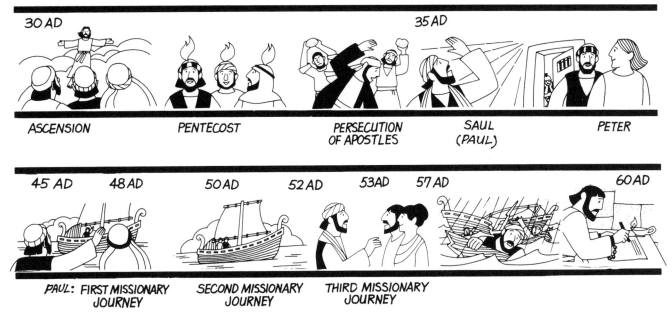

30 AD — ASCENSION   PENTECOST   PERSECUTION OF APOSTLES   35 AD — SAUL (PAUL)   PETER

45 AD   48 AD   50 AD   52 AD   53 AD   57 AD   60 AD

PAUL: FIRST MISSIONARY JOURNEY   SECOND MISSIONARY JOURNEY   THIRD MISSIONARY JOURNEY

Acts

History

Purpose/Theme:

The physician Luke is generally accepted as the author of this record of the establishment and growth of the early church. It emphasizes the presence of the Holy Spirit, the missionary work of Peter and Paul, and how Christianity was not the enemy of the Roman government.

Key Verse:

"But you will receive power when the Holy Spirit comes on you; and you will be my witnesses in Jerusalem, and in all Judea and Samaria, and to the ends of the earth" (1:8).

Outline:

The gospel is preached
☐ in Jerusalem (Acts 1—7)
☐ in Judea and Samaria (Acts 8—12)
☐ to the world (Acts 13—28)

When Events Happened

30 AD — ASCENSION — PENTECOST — PERSECUTION OF APOSTLES — 35 AD — SAUL (PAUL) — PETER

45 AD — 48 AD — PAUL: FIRST MISSIONARY JOURNEY — 50 AD — 52 AD — SECOND MISSIONARY JOURNEY — 53 AD — 57 AD — THIRD MISSIONARY JOURNEY — 60 AD

Countries of People Mentioned at Pentecost

Acts 2:9-11

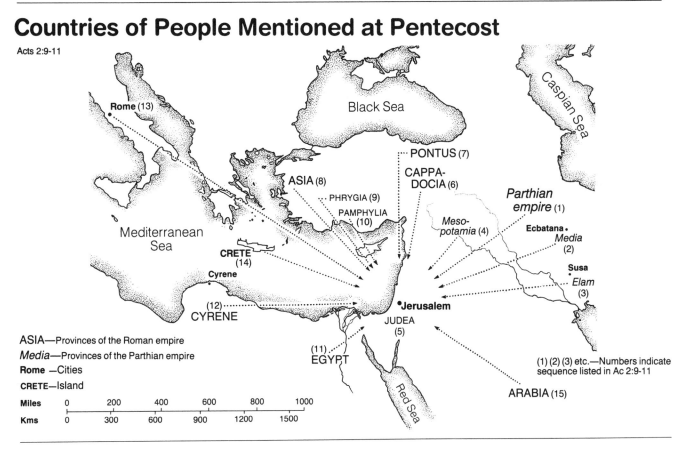

ASIA—Provinces of the Roman empire
Media—Provinces of the Parthian empire
Rome —Cities
CRETE—Island

| Miles | 0 | 200 | 400 | 600 | 800 | 1000 |
| Kms | 0 | 300 | 600 | 900 | 1200 | 1500 |

(1) (2) (3) etc.—Numbers indicate
sequence listed in Ac 2:9-11

Roman Damascus

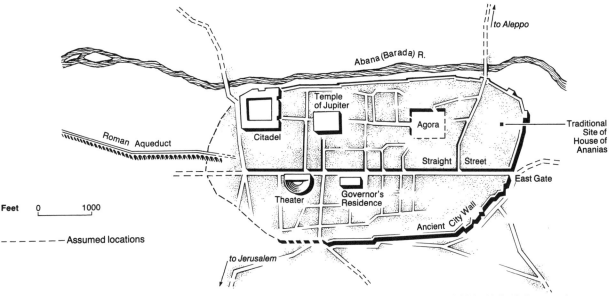

Feet 0   1000

– – – – – Assumed locations

Damascus represented much more to Saul, the strict Pharisee, than another stop on his campaign of repression. It was the hub of a vast commercial network with far-flung lines of caravan trade reaching into north Syria, Mesopotamia, Anatolia, Persia and Arabia. If the new "Way" of Christianity flourished in Damascus, it would quickly reach all these places. From the viewpoint of the Sanhedrin and of Saul, the arch-persecutor, it had to be stopped in Damascus.

The city itself was a veritable oasis, situated in a plain watered by the Biblical rivers Abana and Pharpar.

Roman architecture overlaid the Hellenistic town plan with a great temple to Jupiter and a mile-long colonnaded street, the "Straight Street" of Ac 9:11. The city gates and a section of the town wall may still be seen today, as well as the lengthy bazaar that runs along the line of the ancient street.

The dominant political figure at the time of Paul's escape from Damascus (2 Co 11:32-33) was Aretas IV, king of the Nabateans (9 B.C.-A.D. 40), though normally the Decapolis cities were attached to the province of Syria and were thus under the influence of Rome.

The Spread of the Gospel

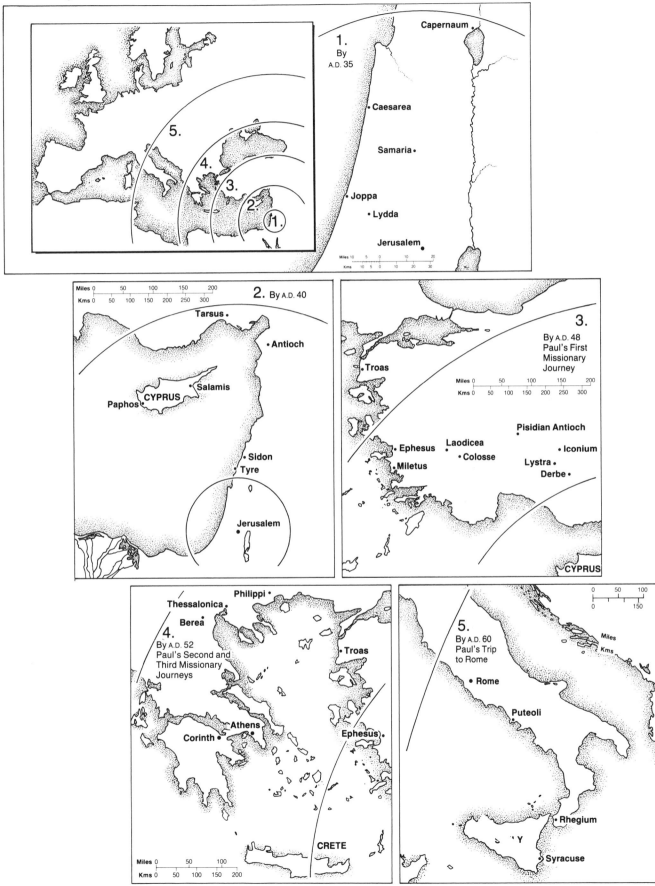

1. By A.D. 35

Capernaum

Caesarea

Samaria

Joppa
Lydda

Jerusalem

Miles 10   5   0   10   20
Kms 10 5 0   10   20   30

2. By A.D. 40

Miles 0   50   100   150   200
Kms 0   50 100 150 200 250 300

Tarsus

Antioch

CYPRUS   Salamis
Paphos

Sidon
Tyre

Jerusalem

3. By A.D. 48
Paul's First Missionary Journey

Miles 0   50   100   150   200
Kms 0   50 100 150 200 250 300

Troas

Pisidian Antioch

Ephesus   Laodicea   Iconium
Miletus   Colosse   Lystra
Derbe

CYPRUS

4. By A.D. 52
Paul's Second and Third Missionary Journeys

Philippi
Thessalonica
Berea

Troas

Athens
Corinth

Ephesus

Miles 0   50   100
Kms 0   50 100 150 200

CRETE

5. By A.D. 60
Paul's Trip to Rome

0   50   100
0   150
Miles
Kms

Rome

Puteoli

Rhegium

Syracuse

© 1989 by Gospel Light Publications. Permission granted to purchaser to reproduce this Sheet for class purposes only.

Paul's First Missionary Journey

Paul's Second Missionary Journey

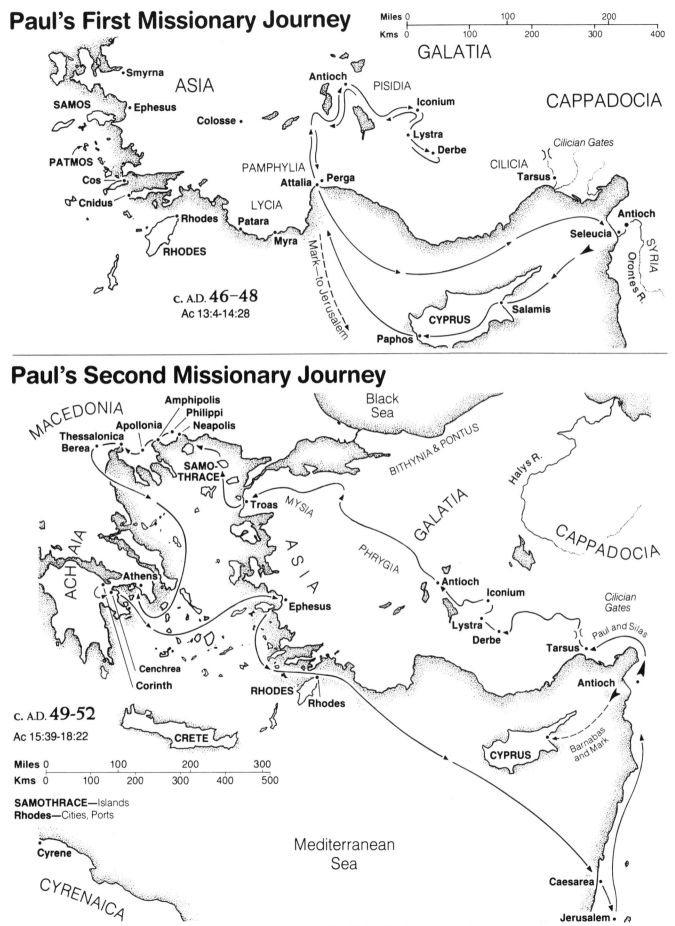

c. A.D. 46-48
Ac 13:4-14:28

c. A.D. 49-52
Ac 15:39-18:22

SAMOTHRACE—Islands
Rhodes—Cities, Ports

Paul's Third Missionary Journey

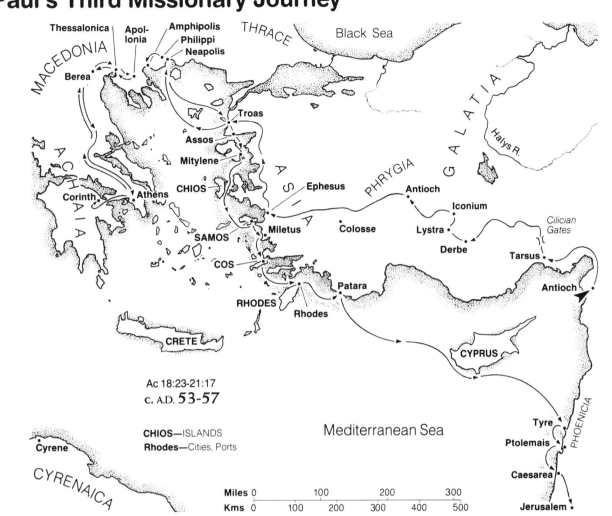

Ac 18:23-21:17
c. A.D. **53-57**

CHIOS—ISLANDS
Rhodes—Cities, Ports

Mediterranean Sea

Miles	0		100		200		300
Kms	0	100	200	300	400	500	

Paul's Journey to Rome

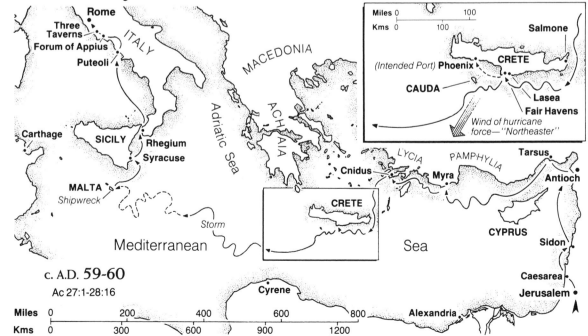

c. A.D. **59-60**

Ac 27:1-28:16

Miles	0		200		400		600		800
Kms	0	300	600	900	1200				

Philip's and Peter's Missionary Journeys

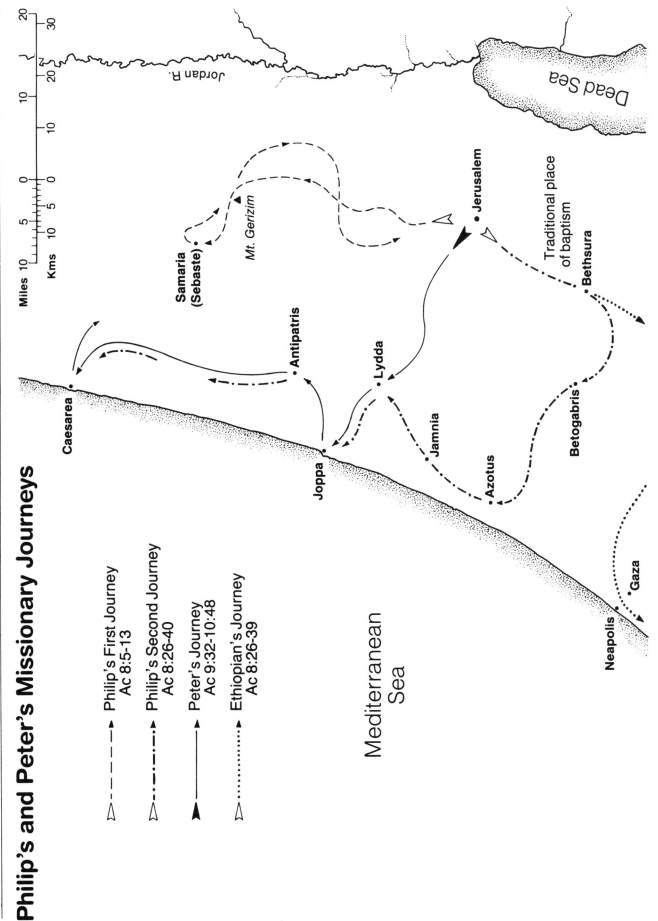

Philip's First Journey
Ac 8:5-13

Philip's Second Journey
Ac 8:26-40

Peter's Journey
Ac 9:32-10:48

Ethiopian's Journey
Ac 8:26-39

Letters by Paul

As early Christianity spread, there was an urgent need for Christians to stay in touch with the teaching of Jesus and the apostles, and to know how to apply it to their lives. This need gave rise to the *Epistles,* or letters, thirteen of which were written by the apostle Paul.

Paul's dramatic conversion is recorded in Acts 9, 22 and 26. His encounter with Jesus transformed him from a persecutor of Christians to the most influential church-planter and letter-writer among first-century Christians.

When Did Paul Write His Letters?

☐ The letters marked ★ were written when Paul was traveling on his missionary journeys.

☐ The letters marked • were written when Paul was a prisoner in Rome at the time of Acts 28.

☐ The letters marked ▲ were written after Paul was freed from the imprisonment we read about in Acts 28. (He was later imprisoned again and killed for preaching about Jesus. Second Timothy was written during this later imprisonment.)

The first nine of Paul's letters were written to groups of believers (churches). The last four were written to three individuals: Timothy, Titus and Philemon.

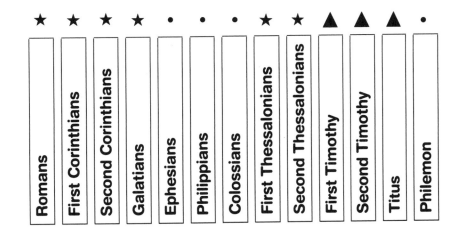

Time Line of Paul's Life

Lines, brackets and dotted lines help show sequence of events, but are not meant to point to precise months or days within a given year, since exact dating is difficult.

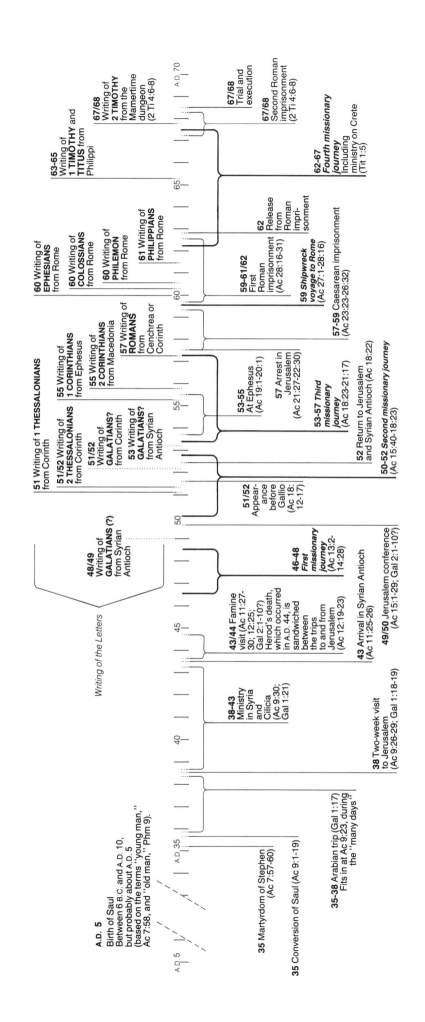

Romans

Letters by Paul

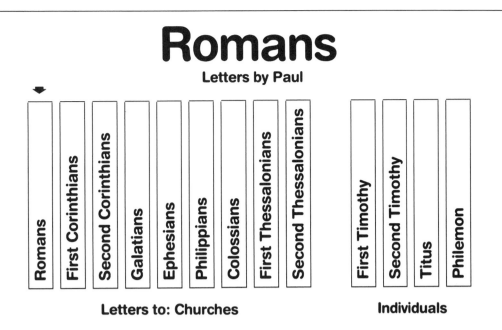

Letters to: Churches   **Individuals**

Purpose/Theme:
☐ Everyone is a sinner and needs God's salvation. God sent His Son Jesus to be our Savior from sin. Those who trust Christ as Savior have their sins forgiven and enjoy eternal life with God.
☐ Israel turned away from Jesus, the Messiah (Savior) God sent. God will still be faithful to His promise, and will restore a remnant.
☐ When we belong to God's family we should live our lives to please Him. We should obey God because we love Him.

Key Verse:
"For all have sinned and fall short of the glory of God, and are justified freely by his grace through the redemption that came by Christ Jesus" (3:23,24).

Outline:
☐ The universal need for grace (Romans 1—4)
☐ Peace and power through grace and the Spirit (Romans 5—8)
☐ Grace for God's Old Testament family (Romans 9—11)
☐ Practical application of the message of grace (Romans 12—16)

When Events Happened

Rome in the Time of Paul

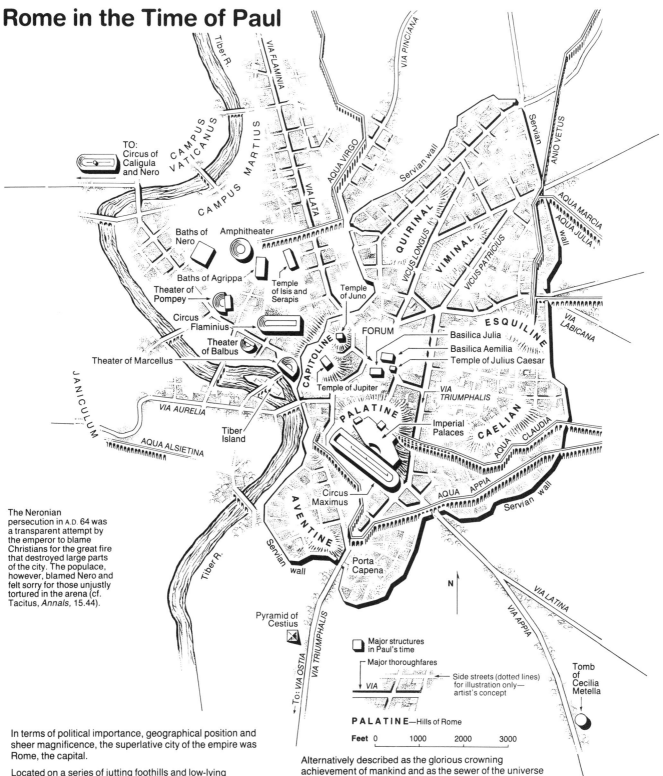

The Neronian persecution in A.D. 64 was a transparent attempt by the emperor to blame Christians for the great fire that destroyed large parts of the city. The populace, however, blamed Nero and felt sorry for those unjustly tortured in the arena (cf. Tacitus, *Annals*, 15.44).

☐ Major structures in Paul's time

┌ Major thoroughfares

↓ *VIA*

Side streets (dotted lines) for illustration only— artist's concept

PALATINE—Hills of Rome

Feet 0   1000   2000   3000

In terms of political importance, geographical position and sheer magnificence, the superlative city of the empire was Rome, the capital.

Located on a series of jutting foothills and low-lying eminences (the "seven hills") east of a bend in the Tiber River some 18 miles from the Mediterranean, Rome was celebrated for its impressive public buildings, aqueducts, baths, theaters and thoroughfares, many of which led from distant provinces. The city of the first Christian century had spread far beyond its fourth-century B.C. "Servian" walls and lay unwalled, secure in its greatness.

The most prominent features were the Capitoline hill, with temples to Jupiter and Juno, and the nearby Palatine, adorned with imperial palaces, including Nero's "Golden House." Both hills overlooked the Roman Forum, the hub of the entire empire.

Alternatively described as the glorious crowning achievement of mankind and as the sewer of the universe where all the scum from every corner of the empire gathered, Rome had reasons for both civic pride in its architecture and shame for staggering urban social problems not unlike those of cities today.

The apostle Paul entered the city from the south on the Via Appia. He first lived under house arrest and then, after a period of freedom, as a condemned prisoner in the Mamertime dungeon near the Forum. Remarkably, Paul was able to proclaim the gospel among all classes of people, from the palace to the prison. According to tradition, he was executed at a spot on the Ostian Way outside Rome in A.D. 68.

1 Corinthians

Letters by Paul

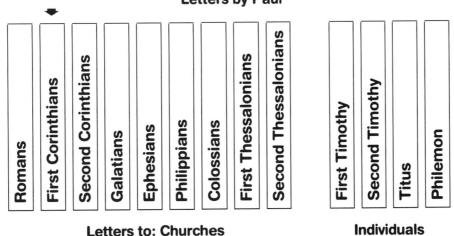

Letters to: Churches **Individuals**

Purpose/Theme:
Paul wrote this letter to the young church at Corinth to curb division, urge morality and encourage them to steadfastness by teaching on the hope of a general resurrection.

Key Verse:
"I appeal to you, brothers, in the name of our Lord Jesus Christ, that all of you agree with one another so that there may be no divisions among you and that you may be perfectly united in mind and thought" (1:10).

Outline:
☐ The importance of unity in Christ (1 Corinthians 1—4)
☐ Personal and public morality (1 Corinthians 5—8)
☐ Influence and Christian freedom (1 Corinthians 9—10)
☐ Worship and spiritual gifts (1 Corinthians 11—14)
☐ The resurrection, and concluding matters (1 Corinthians 15,16)

When Events Happened

▲ = PROBABLE DATE OF WRITING

45 AD   57 58 59   61   66   90   95

PAUL'S MISSIONARY JOURNEYS   ▲ (55)   PRISONER IN ROME (ACTS 28)   SECOND IMPRISONMENT   JOHN

Corinth in the Time of Paul

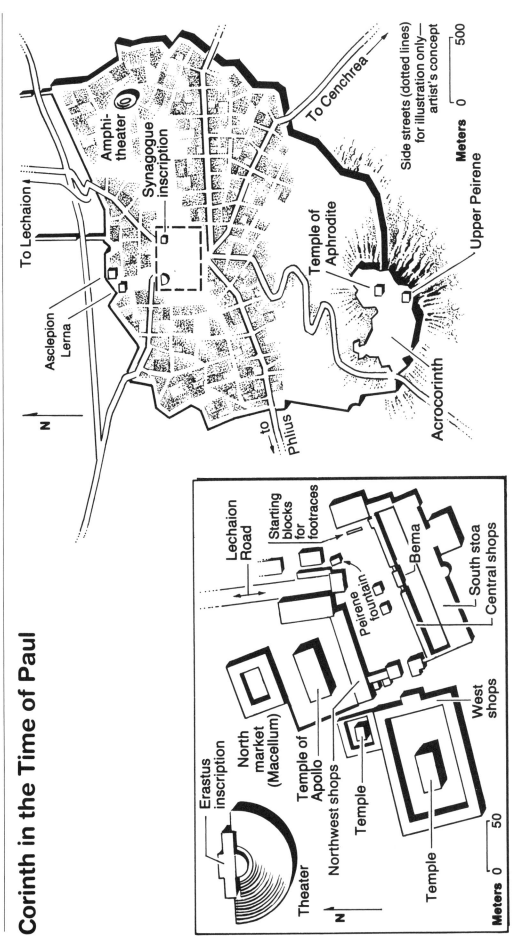

N

To Lechaion

Asclepion
Lerna

Amphi-
theater

Synagogue
inscription

to
Philius

Temple of
Aphrodite

Acrocorinth

To Cenchrea

Upper Peirene

Side streets (dotted lines)
for illustration only—
artist's concept

Meters 0   500

Erastus
inscription

North
market
(Macellum)

Temple of
Apollo

Northwest shops

Temple

Theater

N

Meters 0   50

Lechaion
Road

Starting
blocks
for
footraces

Peirene
fountain

Bema

South stoa
Central shops

West
shops

Temple

The city of Corinth, perched like a one-eyed Titan astride the narrow isthmus connecting the Greek mainland with the Peloponnese, was one of the dominant commercial centers of the Hellenic world as early as the eighth century B.C.

No city in Greece was more favorably situated for land and sea trade. With a high, strong citadel at its back, it lay between the Saronic Gulf and the Ionian Sea and ports at Lechaion and Cenchrea. A *diolkos*, or stone tramway for the overland transport of ships, linked the two seas. Crowning

the Acrocorinth was the temple of Aphrodite, served, according to Strabo, by more than 1,000 pagan priestess-prostitutes.

By the time the gospel reached Corinth in the spring of A.D. 52, the city had a proud history of leadership in the Achaian League, and a spirit of revived Hellenism under Roman domination following the destruction of the city by Mummius in 146 B.C.

Paul's lengthy stay in Corinth brought him directly in contact with the major monuments of the *agora*, many of which still survive. The fountain-house of the spring *Peirene*, the temple of Apollo, the *macellum* or meat market (I Co 10:25), and the theater, the *bema* (Ac 18:12), and the unimpressive synagogue all played a part in the experience of the apostle. An inscription from the theater names the city official Erastus, probably the friend of Paul mentioned in Ro 16:23.

2 Corinthians

Letters by Paul

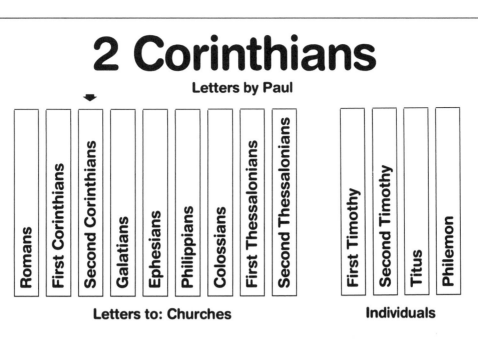

Romans · First Corinthians · Second Corinthians · Galatians · Ephesians · Philippians · Colossians · First Thessalonians · Second Thessalonians

First Timothy · Second Timothy · Titus · Philemon

Letters to: Churches   **Individuals**

Purpose/Theme:
Probably written only a few months after 1 Corinthians, this letter records Paul's response to the result of his earlier writings. Here he defends his authority to correct them, affirms his love for them, and continues to teach on various subjects.

Key Verse:
"We are therefore Christ's ambassadors, as though God were making his appeal through us. We implore you on Christ's behalf: Be reconciled to God" (5:20).

Outline:
☐ Greetings and assurance of concern (2 Corinthians 1—2:13)
☐ Explanation and defense of Paul's ministry (2 Corinthians 2:14—7:16)
☐ The importance of sharing our means with others (2 Corinthians 8—9)
☐ Further defense of Paul's apostleship (2 Corinthians 10—12)
☐ Closing warnings and benediction (2 Corinthians 13)

When Events Happened

▲ = PROBABLE DATE OF WRITING

45AD · 57 · 58 59 · 61 · 66 · 90 · 95

PAUL'S MISSIONARY JOURNEYS · ▲ (55) · PRISONER IN ROME (ACTS 28) · SECOND IMPRISONMENT · JOHN

Galatians

Letters by Paul

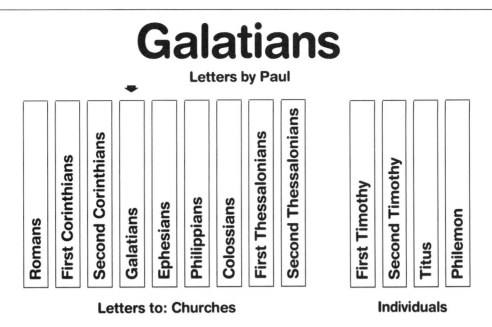

Letters to: Churches   **Individuals**

Purpose/Theme:

Like Romans, the theme of Galatians is salvation by grace through faith—not by keeping the law. The letter was written to be circulated among the churches of Galatia, a Roman province that is now in Turkey.

Key Verse:

"We, too, have put our faith in Christ Jesus that we may be justified by faith in Christ and not by observing the law, because by observing the law no one will be justified" (2:16).

Outline:

☐ Introduction and defense of Paul's authority (Galatians 1—2)
☐ Salvation by grace affirmed and illustrated (Galatians 3—5:15)
☐ Obligations of the grace-full life (Galatians 5:16—6:18)

When Events Happened

Ephesians

Letters by Paul

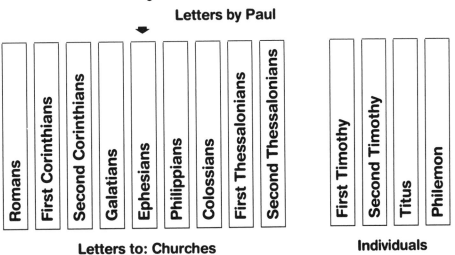

Letters to: Churches   **Individuals**

Purpose/Theme:

Paul wrote this letter, probably from prison in Rome, to affirm Christian unity "in Christ" as a part of God's plan for the ages, and to warn against false doctrine and immorality.

Key Verse:

"God raised us up with Christ and seated us with him in the heavenly realms in Christ Jesus, in order that in the coming ages he might show the incomparable riches of his grace" (2:6,7).

Outline:

☐ The exalted unity of Jew and Gentile in Christ (Ephesians 1—3)
☐ The responsibility of those united in Christ (Ephesians 4:1—6:9)
☐ The Christian's armor, and concluding greetings (Ephesians 6:10-24).

When Events Happened

Ephesians

Ephesus in the Time of Paul

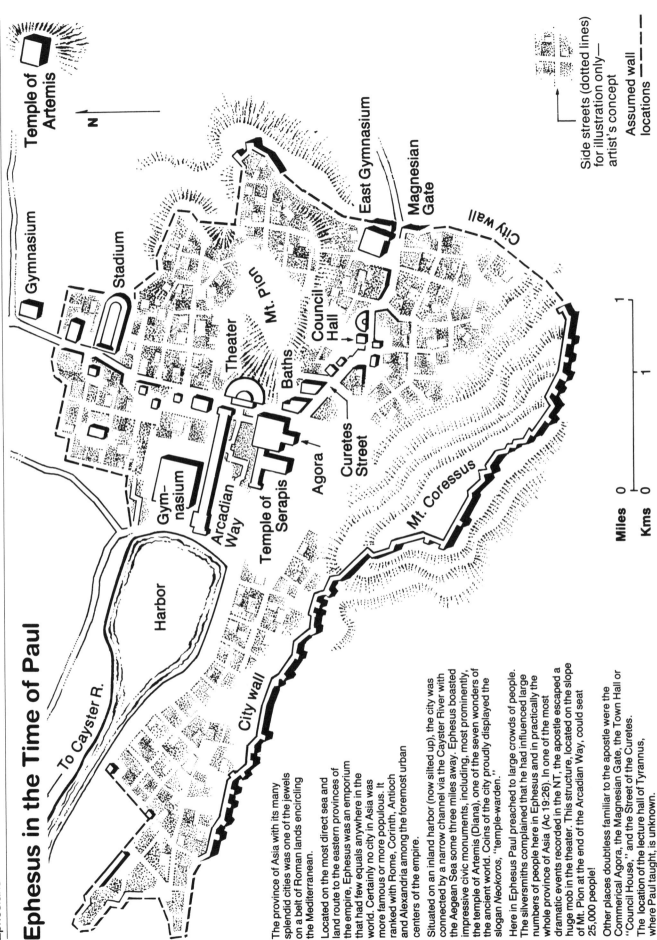

Temple of Artemis

N

Gymnasium

Stadium

Theater

Mt. Pion

East Gymnasium

Magnesian Gate

Council Hall

Baths

City wall

Curetes Street

Agora

Gym-nasium

Arcadian Way

Temple of Serapis

Mt. Coressus

Harbor

To Cayster R.

City wall

Side streets (dotted lines) for illustration only— artist's concept

Assumed wall locations

Miles   0   1

Kms   0   1

The province of Asia with its many splendid cities was one of the jewels on a belt of Roman lands encircling the Mediterranean.

Located on the most direct sea and land route to the eastern provinces of the empire, Ephesus was an emporium that had few equals anywhere in the world. Certainly no city in Asia was more famous or more populous. It ranked with Rome, Corinth, Antioch and Alexandria among the foremost urban centers of the empire.

Situated on an inland harbor (now silted up), the city was connected by a narrow channel via the Cayster River with the Aegean Sea some three miles away. Ephesus boasted impressive civic monuments, including, most prominently, the temple of Artemis (Diana), one of the seven wonders of the ancient world. Coins of the city proudly displayed the slogan *Neokoros,* "temple-warden."

Here in Ephesus Paul preached to large crowds of people. The silversmiths complained that he had influenced large numbers of people here in Ephesus and in practically the whole province of Asia (Ac 19:26). In one of the most dramatic events recorded in the NT, the apostle escaped a huge mob in the theater. This structure, located on the slope of Mt. Pion at the end of the Arcadian Way, could seat 25,000 people!

Other places doubtless familiar to the apostle were the Commerical Agora, the Magnesian Gate, the Town Hall or "Council House," and the Street of the Curetes. The location of the lecture hall of Tyrannus, where Paul taught, is unknown.

Philippians

Letters by Paul

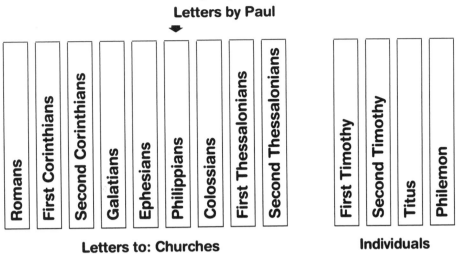

Letters to: Churches　　　　　**Individuals**

Purpose/Theme:

Another "prison epistle," this brief but powerful letter covers a number of issues, with the underlying theme of the importance of joyful faithfulness in the Christian walk, even in the face of suffering.

Key Verses:

"Do not be anxious about anything, but in everything, by prayer and petition, with thanksgiving, present your requests to God. And the peace of God, which transcends all understanding, will guard your hearts and your minds in Christ Jesus" (4:6,7).

Key Thoughts:

☐ God can make negatives turn out positive (Philippians 1:12-19)
☐ The humiliation of Christ as an example (Philippians 2:5-9)
☐ The relative unimportance of fleshly achievement (Philippians 3:1-11)

When Events Happened

Philippi
in the Time of Paul

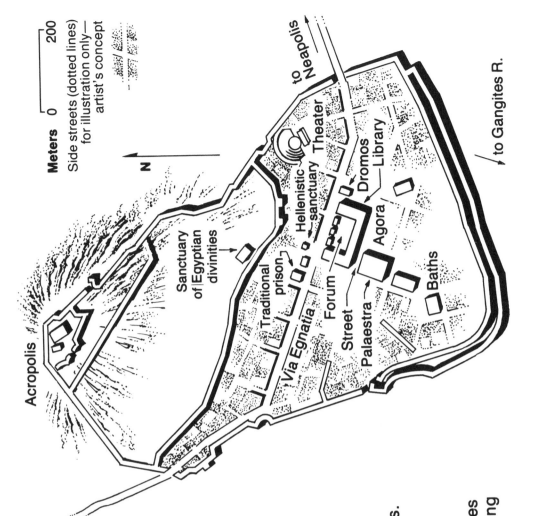

The Roman colony of Philippi (*Colonia Augusta Julia Philippensis*) was an important city in Macedonia, located on the main highway leading from the eastern provinces to Rome. This road, the Via Egnatia, bisected the city's forum and was the chief cause of its prosperity and political importance. Ten miles distant on the coast was Neapolis, the place where Paul landed after sailing from Troas, in response to the Macedonian vision.

As a prominent city of the gold-producing region of Macedonia, Philippi had a proud history. Named originally after Philip II, the father of Alexander the Great, the city was later honored with the name of Julius Caesar and Augustus. Many Italian settlers from the legions swelled the ranks of citizens and made Philippi vigorous and polyglot. It grew from a small settlement to a city of dignity and privilege. Among its highest honors was the *ius Italicum*, by which it enjoyed rights legally equivalent to those of Italian cities.

Ruins of the theater, the acropolis, the forum, the baths, and the western commemorative arch mentioned as the "gate" of the city in Ac 16:13 have been found. A little farther beyond the arch at the Gangites River is the place where Paul addressed some God-fearing women and where Lydia was converted.

Colossians

Letters by Paul

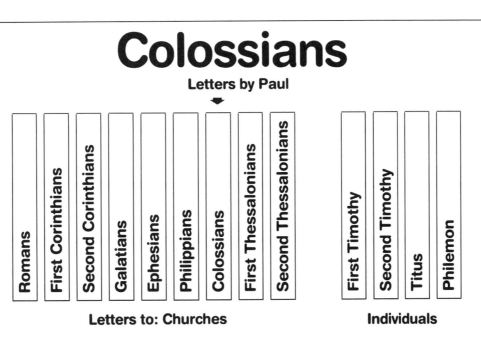

Letters to: Churches   **Individuals**

Purpose/Theme:

Similar to Ephesians, and written about the same time, this letter confronts false doctrine by affirming that Christ must be our doctrinal center, just as he is at the center of Creation.

(The false doctrine at Colosse is often called "gnosticism," a heresy seen in other books of the New Testament as well. Gnosticism was a system of thought that exalted knowledge (gnosis) of certain divine mysteries as the way of salvation. Some forms demanded strict, legal morality, while others thought to "burn out" the flesh with immoral behavior. It could also teach the worship of intermediate beings between heaven and earth. (See Colossians 2:16-23.)

Key Verse:

"See to it that no one takes you captive through hollow and deceptive philosophy, which depends on human tradition and the basic principles of this world rather than on Christ" (2:8).

Key Thoughts:

☐ The kingdom of Christ has a present aspect (Colossians 1:13,14)
☐ The exalted Christ is head of the church (Colossians 1:15-18)
☐ Too many rules and regulations can be bad for spiritual health (2:20-23)
☐ While rule-keeping does not save us, this is no excuse for immorality (3:1-10)

When Events Happened

1 Thessalonians

Letters by Paul

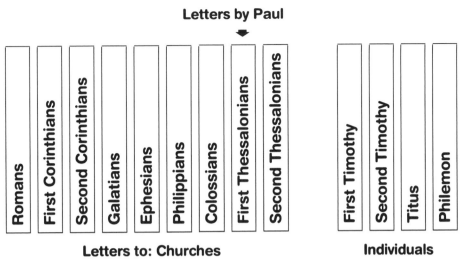

Letters to: Churches   **Individuals**

Purpose/Theme:

Paul wrote this friendly letter to the Christians at Thessalonica only a few months after establishing a congregation there. He writes to confirm their faith, especially in the safety of those who had died in Christ, and to further instruct them on the Second Coming.

Key Verse:

"May [the Lord] strengthen your hearts so that you will be blameless and holy in the presence of our God and Father when our Lord Jesus comes with all his holy ones" (3:13).

Key Thoughts:

☐ Paul's gentle, pastoral behavior (1 Thessalonians 1:7-10
☐ The encouragement faithful Christians are to others (1 Thessalonians 3:6-10)
☐ Instruction about the Second Coming (1 Thessalonians 4:13—5:11)

When Events Happened

▲ =
PROBABLE DATE OF WRITING

45AD   57 58 59   61   66   90   95

PAUL'S MISSIONARY JOURNEYS   ▲(51)   *PRISONER IN ROME (ACTS 28)*   *SECOND IMPRISONMENT*   *JOHN*

2 Thessalonians

Letters by Paul

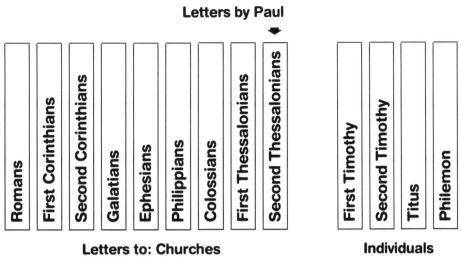

Letters to: Churches   Individuals

Purpose/Theme:
Apparently some Christians in Thessalonica interpreted Paul's first letter to mean that Christ would return so soon that there was no use in working or planning for the future. Paul writes this follow-up note to correct such misunderstandings and to teach further on the subject.

Key Verses:
"The coming of the lawless one will be in accordance with the work of Satan displayed in all kinds of counterfeit miracles, signs and wonders, and in every sort of evil that deceives those who are perishing" (2:9,10).

Key Thoughts:
☐ The "gospel" is not just good news to be believed, but to be obeyed as well (2 Thessalonians 1:8)
☐ Despite the unknown players delaying the Second Coming, a sovereign Lord is in control (2 Thessalonians 2:1-8)
☐ The main responsibility of those who await Christ's coming is to be faithful in order for the Spirit to do His work of sanctification (2 Thessalonians 2:13-15)
☐ Idleness should not be rewarded (2 Thessalonians 3:6-12)

When Events Happened

▲ = PROBABLE DATE OF WRITING

45AD   57   58 59   61   66   90   95

PAUL'S MISSIONARY   ▲(51)   PRISONER IN ROME   SECOND   JOHN
JOURNEYS   (ACTS 28)   IMPRISONMENT

1 Timothy

Letters by Paul

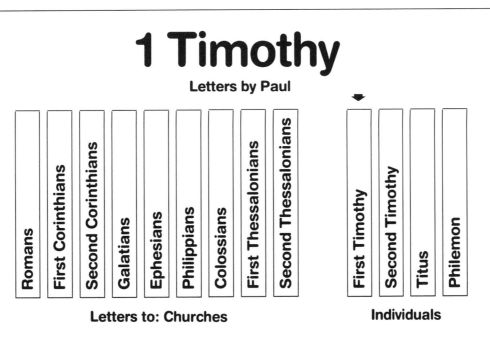

Letters to: Churches   **Individuals**

Purpose/Theme:
The "Pastoral Epistles" earned the name because they show how to "shepherd" the flock of God. Paul was especially concerned, again, about false teachers.

Purpose/Theme:
In 1 Timothy, Paul instructs his younger associate on basic doctrine, church order and personal life.

Key Verses:
"I am writing you these instructions so that, if I am delayed, you will know how people ought to conduct themselves in God's household, which is the church of the living God, the pillar and foundation of the truth" (3:14,15).

Outline:
☐ Greeting, and warning about false teachers (1 Timothy 1)
☐ Instructions on worship (1 Timothy 2)
☐ The qualifications of bishops and deacons (1 Timothy 3)
☐ Warnings and exhortations (1 Timothy 4)
☐ Proper relationships (1 Timothy 5:1—6:2)
☐ Final warnings and benediction (1 Timothy 6:3-21)

When Events Happened

Qualifications for Elders/Overseers and Deacons

Qualification	Role	Reference
Self-controlled	ELDER	1Ti 3:2; Tit 1:8
Hospitable	ELDER	1Ti 3:2; Tit 1:8
Able to teach	ELDER	1Ti 3:2; 5:17; Tit 1:9
Not violent but gentle	ELDER	1Ti 3:3; Tit 1:7
Not quarrelsome	ELDER	1Ti 3:3
Not a lover of money	ELDER	1Ti 3:3
Not a recent convert	ELDER	1Ti 3:6
Has a good reputation with outsiders	ELDER	1Ti 3:7
Not overbearing	ELDER	Tit 1:7
Not quick-tempered	ELDER	Tit 1:7
Loves what is good	ELDER	Tit 1:8
Upright, holy	ELDER	Tit 1:8
Disciplined	ELDER	Tit 1:8
Above reproach (blameless)	ELDER / DEACON	1Ti 3:2; Tit 1:6 / 1Ti 3:9
Husband of one wife	ELDER / DEACON	1Ti 3:2; Tit 1:6 / 1Ti 3:12
Temperate	ELDER / DEACON	1Ti 3:2; Tit 1:7 / 1Ti 3:8
Respectable	ELDER / DEACON	1Ti 3:2 / 1Ti 3:8
Not given to drunkenness	ELDER / DEACON	1Ti 3:3; Tit 1:7 / 1Ti 3:8
Manages his own family well	ELDER / DEACON	1Ti 3:4 / 1Ti 3:12
Sees that his children obey him	ELDER / DEACON	1Ti 3:4-5; Tit 1:6 / 1Ti 3:12
Does not pursue dishonest gain	ELDER / DEACON	Tit 1:7 / 1Ti 3:8
Keeps hold of the deep truths	ELDER / DEACON	Tit 1:9 / 1Ti 3:9
Sincere	DEACON	1Ti 3:8
Tested	DEACON	1Ti 3:10

Paul's Fourth Missionary Journey

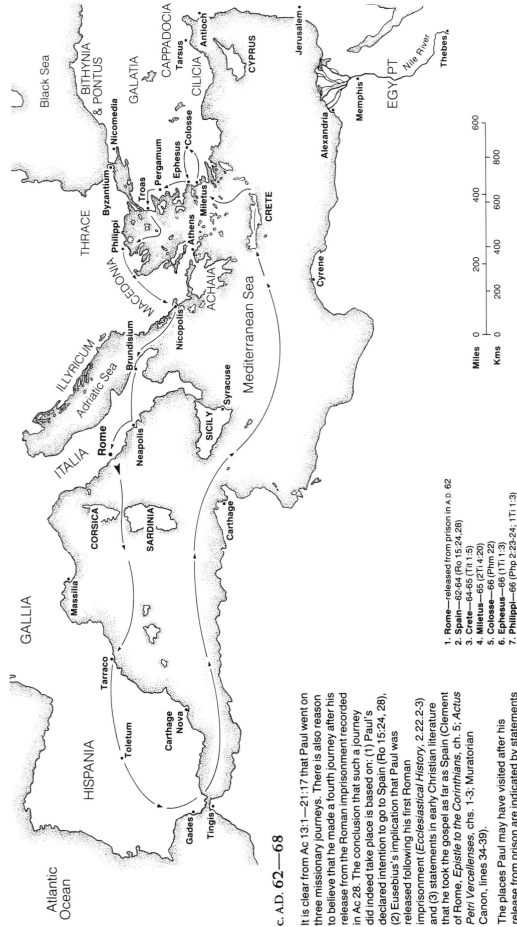

c. A.D. 62—68

It is clear from Ac 13:1—21:17 that Paul went on three missionary journeys. There is also reason to believe that he made a fourth journey after his release from the Roman imprisonment recorded in Ac 28. The conclusion that such a journey did indeed take place is based on: (1) Paul's declared intention to go to Spain (Ro 15:24, 28), (2) Eusebius's implication that Paul was released following his first Roman imprisonment (*Ecclesiastical History*, 2.22.2-3) and (3) statements in early Christian literature that he took the gospel as far as Spain (Clement of Rome, *Epistle to the Corinthians*, ch. 5; *Actus Petri Vercellenses*, chs. 1-3; Muratorian Canon, lines 34-39).

The places Paul may have visited after his release from prison are indicated by statements of intention in his earlier writings and by subsequent mention in the Pastoral Letters. The order of his travel cannot be determined with certainty, but the itinerary at the right seems likely.

1. **Rome**—released from prison in A.D. 62
2. **Spain**—62-64 (Ro 15:24,28)
3. **Crete**—64-65 (Tit 1:5)
4. **Miletus**—65 (2Ti 4:20)
5. **Colosse**—66 (Phm 22)
6. **Ephesus**—66 (1Ti 1:3)
7. **Philippi**—66 (Php 2:23-24; 1Ti 1:3)
8. **Nicopolis**—66-67 (Tit 3:12)
9. **Rome**—67
10. Martyrdom—67/68

2 Timothy

Letters by Paul

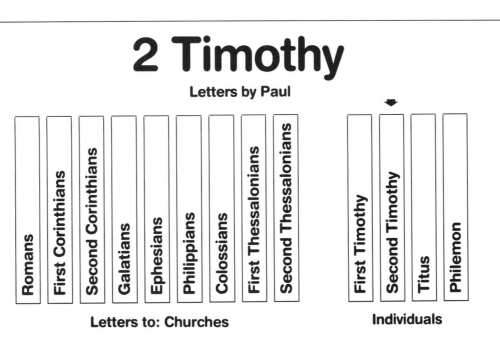

Letters to: Churches   **Individuals**

Purpose/Theme:

This is quite possibly Paul's last letter. There is evidence that after his first imprisonment in Rome (see Acts 28) he was released, went on another missionary journey, then was jailed in Rome again. It is thought that 2 Timothy was written then, as a message of encouragement for Timothy to carry on the faith.

Key Verses:

"I have fought the good fight, I have finished the race, I have kept the faith. Now there is in store for me the crown of righteousness, which the Lord, the righteous Judge, will award to me on that day—and not only to me, but also to all who have longed for his appearing" (4:7,8).

Key Thoughts:

☐ Paul's personal relationship with Timothy and with the Lord (2 Timothy 1:3-12)
☐ Exhortation to be faithful (2 Timothy 2)
☐ Warnings against ungodliness (2 Timothy 3:1-9)
☐ The inspiration of Scripture (2 Timothy 3:16-17)
☐ A commission to preach the Word (2 Timothy 4:1-5)

When Events Happened

Titus

Letters by Paul

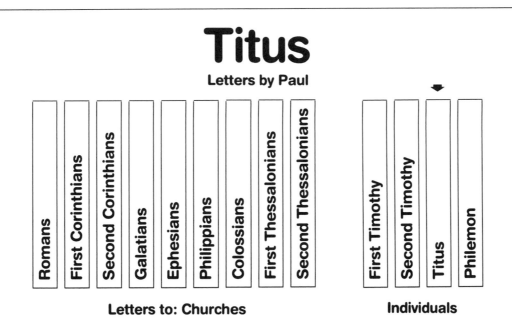

Letters to: Churches   **Individuals**

Purpose/Theme:
Paul may have written this letter to another younger minister, Titus, from the Roman prison about the same time as 1 Timothy. Here he gives additional teaching about pastoral duties, and warnings against ungodliness.

Key Verses:
"The grace of God that brings salvation has appeared to all men. It teaches us to say 'No' to ungodliness and worldly passions, and to live self-controlled, upright and godly lives" (2:11,12).

Key Thoughts:
☐ More instructions on the qualifications of elders (Titus 1:5-9)
☐ The importance of sound morals (Titus 1:10-15)
☐ The importance of sound doctrine and godly relationships (Titus 2)

When Events Happened

Philemon

Letters by Paul

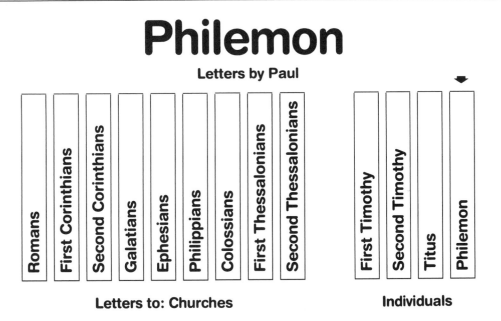

Romans | First Corinthians | Second Corinthians | Galatians | Ephesians | Philippians | Colossians | First Thessalonians | Second Thessalonians

First Timothy | Second Timothy | Titus | Philemon

Letters to: Churches   **Individuals**

Purpose/Theme:

This personal letter from Paul to his friend Philemon reveals some interesting facts about the times. A slave named Onesimus had run away from his master, Philemon, and had joined Paul at Rome. Now Paul asks Philemon to set Onesimus free and to accept him as a brother in Christ.

Key Verse:

"I pray that you may be active in sharing your faith, so that you will have a full understanding of every good thing we have in Christ" (vs. 6).

When Events Happened

▲ = PROBABLE DATE OF WRITING

45 AD   57 58 59   61   66   90   95

PAUL'S MISSIONARY JOURNEYS   PRISONER IN ROME (ACTS 28) ▲ (60)   SECOND IMPRISONMENT   JOHN

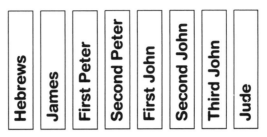

General Letters

These letters (or "epistles") are called "General" because they are addressed to a more general readership than others, such as Paul's letter to the Galatians. Most are also named after their author, instead of their audience.

You may find that this list differs from some older lists which include the book of Hebrews as one of Paul's letters. Most modern scholars now believe that the author of Hebrews is unknown. Also, since it addresses not a specific church but Jewish Christians throughout the world, it is included here with the General Letters.

When Events Happened:

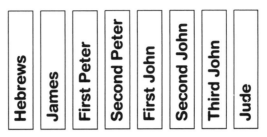

45AD   57 58 59   61   66   90   95

PAUL'S MISSIONARY JOURNEYS — PRISONER IN ROME (ACTS 28) — SECOND IMPRISONMENT — JOHN

Hebrews
General Letters

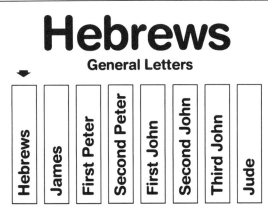

Purpose/Theme:
The book of Hebrews was written to encourage Jewish Christians to affirm their place in Christ instead of returning to the Old Law. It shows that Christ is greater than the prophets, the angels, Moses, Joshua and the Jewish priesthood.

Key Verse:
"In the past God spoke to our forefathers through the prophets at many times and in various ways, but in these last days he has spoken to us by his Son" (1:1).

Outline:
☐ Christ is greater than the angels (Hebrews 1—2)
☐ He is greater than Moses (Hebrews 3)
☐ The real "Sabbath rest" was not ushered in by the Old Covenant, but is promised under Christ (Hebrews 4:1-13)
☐ Christ is greater than the priesthood and all older covenants (Hebrews 4:14—10:18)
☐ Therefore, have faith and persevere! (Hebrews 10:19—13:25)

When Events Happened:

James
General Letters

Hebrews	James	First Peter	Second Peter	First John	Second John	Third John	Jude

Purpose/Theme:
Like the book of Proverbs, James is full of practical wisdom and rules for right living. It was probably written by the James who was Jesus' half-brother.

Key Verses:
"Do not merely listen to the word, and so deceive yourselves. Do what it says" (1:22).
"Faith by itself, if it is not accompanied by action, is dead" (2:17).

Key Thoughts:
☐ The growth potential in trials (James 1:3-4,12)
☐ The evolution of sin (James 1:13-15)
☐ The folly of favoritism (James 2:1-13)
☐ Taming the tongue (James 1:26; 3:1-12)
☐ Friendship with the world (James 4:1-12)
☐ The prayer of faith (James 5:13-20)

When Events Happened

PROBABLY WRITTEN BEFORE A.D. 60

45AD   57 58 59   61   66   90   95

PAUL'S MISSIONARY JOURNEYS   PRISONER IN ROME (ACTS 28)   SECOND IMPRISONMENT   JOHN

1 Peter

General Letters

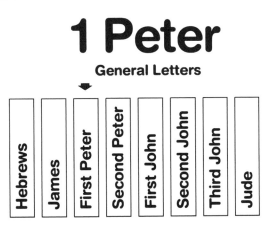

Purpose/Theme:

This inspirational letter from the apostle Peter was written to strengthen early Christians who were being persecuted for their faith. If "Babylon" (5:13) stood for Rome, as was common in the early church, Peter was in Rome when he wrote this letter.

Key Verses:

"If you are insulted because of the name of Christ, you are blessed . . . . If you suffer as a Christian, do not be ashamed, but praise God that you bear that name" (4:14,16).

Key Thoughts:

☐ Suffering refines faith like refining purifies gold (1 Peter 1:6,7; see also 3:13-17; 4:12-19)
☐ Our holy calling calls for holy living (1 Peter 1:13-25)
☐ Christians are the new priesthood (1 Peter 2:9)
☐ Teaching on right relationships (1 Peter 2:1—3:7)
☐ The use of spiritual gifts (1 Peter 4:9-11)

When Events Happened

PROBABLY WRITTEN IN EARLY 60S

45AD   57 5859   61   66   90   95

PAUL'S MISSIONARY JOURNEYS   PRISONER IN ROME (ACTS 28)   SECOND IMPRISONMENT   JOHN

2 Peter

General Letters

Hebrews	James	First Peter	Second Peter	First John	Second John	Third John	Jude

Purpose/Theme:

Second Peter has the ring of an Old Testament prophet predicting doom for those who oppose God in unrighteousness and urging faithfulness in the face of the soon-coming Day of the Lord.

Key Verse:

"The Lord is not slow in keeping his promise, as some understand slowness. He is patient with you, not wanting anyone to perish, but everyone to come to repentance" (3:9).

Key Thoughts:

☐ Growing in the Christian graces (2 Peter 1:5-9)
☐ Biblical prophecy is inspired (2 Peter 1:19-21)
☐ Warning against false teachers (2 Peter 2)
☐ What to make of the delayed return of Christ (2 Peter 3)

When Events Happened

PROBABLY WRITTEN BETWEEN 65-68

45 AD   57 58 59   61   66   90   95

PAUL'S MISSIONARY JOURNEYS   PRISONER IN ROME (ACTS 28)   SECOND IMPRISONMENT   JOHN

1 John
2 John
3 John

General Letters

Hebrews	James	First Peter	Second Peter	First John	Second John	Third John	Jude

Purpose/Theme:

Apparently 1, 2 and 3 John were written by the apostle John (the John who also wrote the Gospel of John) in his old age. They were first circulated in and around the city of Ephesus. Their theme is love and light, good and evil, and how to stay free of "gnostic" influences (see note at Ephesians).

Notice that 2 John is addressed to "a chosen lady." It is likely that this refers to a church in the area, rather than to a special woman.

Third John is addressed to a man named "Gaius," who is warned about a local church leader, Diotrephes, "who loves to be first" (vs. 9).

Key Verse in 1 John:

"My dear children, I write this to you so that you will not sin. But if anybody does sin, we have one who speaks to the Father in our defense—Jesus Christ, the Righteous One (2:1).

Outline of 1 John:

☐ Walking in the light (1 John 1—2:17)
☐ Warning against antichrist (1 John 2:18-27)
☐ Living as God's children (1 John 2:28—3:24)
☐ Warnings against worldliness (1 John 4)
☐ The importance of faith (1 John 5)

Key Verses in 2 John:

"I am not writing you a new command but one we have had from the beginning. I ask that we love one another. And this is love: that we walk in obedience to his commands" (vss. 5,6).

Key Thoughts in 2 John:

☐ Walking in love (2 John 4-6)
☐ Warning against deceivers (2 John 7-11)

Key verse in 3 John:

"I pray that you may enjoy good health and that all may go well with you, even as your soul is getting along well" (3 John 2).

Key Thought in 3 John:

☐ Church leadership must be out of higher motives than personal ambition
(3 John 9-10)

When Events Happened

Jude

General Letters

Hebrews	James	First Peter	Second Peter	First John	Second John	Third John	Jude

Purpose/Theme:
The Jude who was the Lord's half-brother may have written this as a general letter warning of falling away from the truth. It is very similar to 2 Peter in its strong prophetic warnings.

Key Verses:
"In the last times there will be scoffers who will follow their own ungodly desires. These are the men who divide you, who follow mere natural instincts and do not have the Spirit" (Jude 18,19).

Key Thoughts
☐ False teachers face sobering judgment (Jude 5-16)
☐ Doubters come in several forms; believers must make a distinction (Jude 22,23).

When Events Happened

PROBABLY WRITTEN BETWEEN 65-68

45AD   57 58 59   61   66   90   95

PAUL'S MISSIONARY JOURNEYS   PRISONER IN ROME (ACTS 28)   SECOND IMPRISONMENT   JOHN

Prophecy

Revelation

Although Revelation is the only book of prophecy in our New Testament, it is very much like some Old Testament prophecies. It is also similar to writings that were produced between the Testaments.

In other words, this style of writing was very popular in ancient times. For us, interpreting their symbols, numbers and imagery can be very controversial. Perhaps ancient readers were more familiar with what the symbols stood for.

Revelation

Prophecy

Revelation

Purpose/Theme:

Once more, tradition holds that we are treated to the writings of the elderly apostle John. He paints breathtaking pictures of the war between good and evil, in the visionary style of Ezekiel's prophecy. His purpose is to strengthen Christians who face persecution by showing them the glorious victory awaiting the faithful.

Key Verse:

"They will make war against the Lamb, but the Lamb will overcome them because he is Lord of lords and King of kings—and with him will be his called, chosen, and faithful followers" (17:14).

Outline:

☐ Introduction (Revelation 1)
☐ Letters to the seven churches of Asia (Revelation 2—3)
☐ Visions of heaven (Revelation 4—5)
☐ The seven seals (Revelation 6—7)
☐ The seven trumpets (Revelation 8—11)
☐ Signs of the end (Revelation 12—14)
☐ The seven bowls of wrath (Revelation 15—16)
☐ The fate of Babylon, or Rome (Revelation 17—18)
☐ The victorious Christ (Revelation 19—20)
☐ The holy city (Revelation 21:1—22:6)
☐ Concluding blessings and cursings (Revelation 22:8-21)

When Events Happened